WRITING OUR WAY OUT OF THE DARK

WRITING OUR WAY OUT OF THE DARK

AN ANTHOLOGY BY CHILD ABUSE SURVIVORS

EDITED BY
ELIZABETH CLAMAN

QSP Queen of Swords Press
LITERARY ACTS OF BRAVERY

Queen of Swords Press gratefully acknowledges a grant from Oregon's Literay Arts which helped pay the printing costs for this anthology.

Editor Elizabeth Claman also wishes to thank Drs. Russell Colgin, Barbara Zelwer, Gladys Bennett, Gisela Bergman, Suzanne Schumann, and Blu Wagner for their invaluable therapeutic interventions over the past twenty-five years. This book is dedicated to them.

Special thanks to Blu Wagner for exceptional feedback on the manuscript for this anthology.

❖ ❖ ❖

Cover painting, "Daddy Enraged," 60"x 56" (detail), by Jane Orleman. An exhibit of her paintings is available nationally through the Exhibit Touring Service (1-800-356-1256).

Book design by Elizabeth Claman and Cheryl McLean
Typesetting by ImPrint Services, Corvallis, Oregon.

Published in the United States by Queen of Swords Press,
PO Box 3646, Eugene, Oregon 97403

Library of Congress Catalog Card Number: 95-68828

ISBN 0-9638992-2-8 (paper)

Printed in the U.S.A

WRITING OUR WAY OUT OF THE DARK

The title of this collection carries a dual meaning.

Child abuse has too long been a dark, hidden secret.
By writing, survivors bring their painful experiences to light.

Too, darkness often envelops the lives of child abuse victims,
blotting out their feelings of self-worth or personal power.
By writing, survivors begin to emerge from the dark and to heal.

TABLE OF CONTENTS

EDITOR'S FOREWORD

Ever since 1986, when I first read Laura Davis and Ellen Bass's book, *The Courage to Heal: A Guide for Women Survivors of Childhood Sexual Abuse*, and heard Dorianne Laux read her powerful poems about incest, I have been using poetry to heal from my own childhood violations. Noting the powerful effect, I knew there must be other writers growing toward healing by the power of the word. Having long wanted to know who they were and how they were using their art for healing, in the spring of 1994 I put out a call for manuscripts on the subject and was deluged with submissions. One of the most difficult tasks I have ever performed was selecting the works to include in this anthology, and deciding which ones I had to send back, regretfully, to their authors. All of the contributors to this book—like those whose writings were not accepted here for publication—strike me as deeply brave. I know how difficult it is to write one's hard truths, and then send them out to strangers, risking rejection. I commend each of the writers who did so, and dedicate this book to all of you.

Not long ago at a poetry reading for International Women's Day in Portland, Oregon, several of the contributors to this anthology and I shared some of our writing with an audience of about twenty women and men. Afterward I opened the floor for comments from the audience, and poet Sharon Doubiago—who later that afternoon would read "Outlaw" (a poem I fell in love with and will use in the sequel to this anthology)—asked if I had seen a recent *AWP (Associated Writing Programs)* article calling for "No more incest poems." I said that I had not, but that it decidedly merited a letter to the editor, whereupon a woman in the second row, whom I recognized from earlier comments as a survivor, burst out, "What about 'No more incest!'" The audience and some of the anthology contributors applauded her outrage. Participants in the forum went on to say that efforts to silence this kind of writing, or even to demand of it some image of easy healing and resolution, is a kind of censorship that we as writers and as survivors cannot tolerate. I heartily agree. We must continue to tell our stories, refusing to be silenced or censored for as long as children are at risk.

The poems, stories, and essays in this anthology are the uncensored outpourings of women and men who have been profoundly hurt by the violence that permeates our families. They are not easy works to read. The first part of the book, "This Gun is Real: What We Know to be True," contains some graphic descriptions of abuse which are extremely painful. If they raise painful memories for you as you read, I urge you to find someone to talk to about your feelings. You might want to share this book with others in a support group, or with a therapist. There is a resource directory in the back, which I encourage you to use. Don't remain isolated with your pain!

In the second section, "From My Window, I See Mountains: The Journey Toward Healing," writers have shared some of their strategies for recovery, and moments along the way toward healing. But there are no quick fixes. The writings you will read on the issue of healing are clearly part of a process; they do not mark a final destination point at which the survivor can blithely say, "Aha! Now I'm all better!" However, as many survivors can and do attest, the journey can include compassion, insight, humor and a sensitivity to beauty that make life seem miraculous.

There is one more essential note to bear in mind while reading this book. It was underscored for me in a letter from the fine counselor and children's advocate, Jan Hindman, who wrote, "Trauma is unique to each individual in recovery. There have been many times in the last 21 years [the duration of Hindman's practice] when sexual abuse victims have read the statements of others and discounted themselves, [thinking] 'What happened to me wasn't that bad, therefore I shouldn't be suffering.'" It is my concern as editor of this book that no one have such an experience. Like Jan Hindman, I feel very strongly that survivors should not compare themselves with others, but should be encouraged to find safety in knowing that they are not alone. One of the most important goals of this anthology is to offer a sense of community to people who were hurt as children. Compiling it has definitely given me such a sense.

Finally, this anthology has another goal as well. It is my wish that across the United States and around the world reading it might move people who have been hurt to express themselves, to pick up their pens, paint brushes, and sculpting tools, to slip on their dancing shoes, to tune up their voice or their violin, so as to use the spark that is in every one of us as an instrument of healing. May it help all of you who read it to find inspiration among its voices, to experience catharsis and renewal, to discover new ways to release past hurts and move onward by the power of your own inalienable creativity.

It is in this spirit I offer you *Writing Our Way Out of the Dark: An Anthology by Child Abuse Survivors.*

Elizabeth Claman
June 1995

PART I — THIS GUN IS REAL
WHAT WE KNOW TO BE TRUE

Pain is important: how we evade it, how we succumb to it, how we deal with it, how we transcend it.

—Audre Lorde

You can enhance the pleasure of life by meeting and experiencing the pain first and getting it over with.

—M. Scott Peck

Amanda Powell

FREUD'S BACK

Now that I know what I know:
what I knew, but couldn't remember,
stumbling out away from it back then at twenty
                    as from a wreck
and flailing and grasping toward you;
and what you knew, but couldn't credit
being strangely in this, oh, one instance loyal
to your sex—the one time, winter evening train
traveling back to college, I tried
to tell you about my father in my childhood bed but I
was trying to say the bedsag   the gutshock   wakening the hand
under the covers and then the worst, the nothing,
as a blind, nailed, knuckled, stale after-shave hand
          might come through this night
not just to wreck us along with a trainload of strangers but
to pluck this train from the track and the track from
                                                            Connecticut—

what did you know, the train barreled nosy and unfeeling along
and you said, "Well, you know
what Freud said about that." Wish-fulfillment,
you actually said
back then when I loved you,

so that later at the fluorescent heart of that same snowy dark
in the university Science Center library ladies' room I thought
that I knew I was quite mad—and I mean crazy—
that I would shrivel and die,
                    my young green face in the mirror said so,
I left you there at your evening job meticulously shelving books
and went home to drink;
but still some tiny girlish part of myself
let's hear it   knew what I knew.

And now we know
that Freud knew too, early on, what he knew:
what my father had done, those Viennese fathers, to those girls
              grown women,

and he, Freud, turned his back on it,
on his lonely and scorned knowledge, and so
on honor and science.

I can see it now, Freud's back—
the little specifying moles, sparse hairs, the ribs
just showing there above the kidneys, under his aging
flesh—see it as a wife might shy from it, turning
to put away some real object of the solid doctor's
in the open-mouthed bureau; *not* letting herself know
that she is thinking, glimpsing the innocent
blind knobs of two lumbar vertebrae as the
                    undershirt covers them,
so like the children's sentient spines when they were small—
thinking how small he is, really, though she knows not
                    the half of it,
how ponderously little he will let himself know.

Barbara Hendryson

STARS

> *Suffer the first vision that set*
> *fire to the stars*
> —Dylan Thomas

The girl does acrobatics on the front lawn.
A sharp brief rain has just passed over
leaving the silvery clouds of steam it has drawn

from the asphalt. It is Houston, summer, the lazy
interim that follows the end of war.
She does a few cartwheels, tries to perfect

her back-bend, fingers straining for grass,
the solid earth. She looks to be nearly eight
and tall for her age; something almost adult

about her, a certain cast to her eyes, as if they have
witnessed a piece of her future before she will
come to it. Her hair is dark, exotic, permed

to curl gracefully near her face and down the strong
V of her back. In a few years, she could be
a glossy likeness staring out from the darkness
of a boy's locker, or the slit of a mirror frame.
But now she retreats, almost carefree, to the shade
of the porch steps. She watches a man amble out

of the house. He is tall, loosely arranged, moving
on a strange gait, as if drunk or still asleep.
He bends to her—the father now. He opens

her hand to receive his gift, a barrette of three
white stars. She smiles, nods up at him.
He lifts her hair. Accordingly, she clips

the loose mane of her curls back from her face.
Later, he will trace for her the early stars,
the hot terrestrial planets that revolve

around the sun, the necessary magnitude
of their fires. But now, it is still afternoon
and his fatherly ways preside over his acts

of kindness, the way he regards the face of his daughter,
sees to the nourishment of her child's body,
her flyaway hair. Whereas, at night there will be

a different order: His cadenced steps to her bed.
A merciful blanket of darkness. The chamber of fire
from which she, alone, will emerge and shine.

Dorianne Laux

TWO PICTURES OF MY SISTER

If an ordinary person is silent,
this may be a tactical maneuver.
If a writer is silent, this is lying.
—Jaroslav Seifert

The pose is stolen from Monroe, struck
in the sun's floodlight, eyes lowered,
a long-stemmed plastic rose between her teeth.
My cast off bathing suit hangs
in folds over her ribs, straps
cinched, pinned at the back of her neck.
Barefoot on the hot cement, knock-kneed,
comical if it weren't for the graceful
angles of her arms, her flesh soft
against the chipped stucco.

The other picture is in my head.
It is years later.
It is in color.
Blond hair curls away from the planes of her face
like wood shavings.
She wears a lemon-yellow ruffled top, denim
cut-offs, her belly button squeezed to a slit
above the silver snap.
She stands against the hallway wall
while Dad shakes his belt in her face.
A strip of skin has been peeled
from her bare shoulder, there are snake
lines across her thighs, a perfect curl
around her long neck.
She looks through him
as if she could see behind his head.
She dares him.
Go on. Hit me again.

He lets the folded strap unravel to the floor.
Holds it by its tail. Bells the buckle
off her cheekbone.

She does not move or cry or even wince
as the welt blooms on her temple
like a flower opening frame by frame
in a nature film.
It lowers her eyelid with its violet petals
and as he walks away only her eyes
move, like the eyes of a portrait that follow you
around a museum room, her face
a stubborn moon that trails the car all night,
stays locked in the frame of the back window
no matter how many turns you take,
no matter how far you go.

WHAT MY FATHER TOLD ME

Always I have done what I was asked.
Melmac dishes stacked on rag towels.
The slack of a vacuum cleaner cord
wound around my hand. Laundry
hung on a line.
There is always much to do and I do it.
The iron resting in its frame, hot
in the shallow pan of summer
as the basins of his hands push
aside the book I am reading.
I do as I am told, hold his penis
like the garden hose, in this bedroom,
in the bathroom, over the toilet
or my bare stomach.
I do the chores, pull weeds out back,
finger stink-bug husks, snail carcasses,
pile dead grass in black bags. At night
his feet are safe on their pads, light
on the wall-to-wall as he takes
the hallway to my room.
His voice, the hiss of lawn sprinklers,
the wet hush of sweat in his hollows,
the mucus still damp
in the corners of my eyes as I wake.

Summer ends. Schoolwork doesn't suit me.
My fingers unaccustomed to the slimness
of a pen, the delicate touch it takes
to uncoil the mind.
History. A dateline pinned to the wall.
Beneath each president's face, a quotation.
Pictures of buffalo and wheatfields,
a wagon train circled for the night,
my hand raised to ask the question,
Where did the children sleep?

QUARTER TO SIX

and the house swept with the colors of dusk,
I set the table with plates and lace. In these minutes
left to myself, before the man and child scuff at the doorstep
and come in, I think of you and wonder what I would say
if I could write. Would I tell you how I avoid his eyes,
this man I've learned to live with, afraid
of what he doesn't know about me. That I've finished
a pack of cigarettes in one sitting, to ready myself
for dinner, when my hands will waver over a plate of fish
as my daughter grows up normal in the chair beside me. Missy,

this is what's become of the wedding you swore you'd come to
wearing black. That was in 1970 as we sat on the bleached
floor of the sanitarium sharing a cigarette you'd won
in a game of pool. You said even school was better
than this ward, where they placed the old men
in their draped pants, the housewives screaming in loud
flowered shifts as they clung to the doors that lined the halls.
When we ate our dinner of fish and boiled potatoes,
it was you who nudged me under the table
as the thin man in striped pajamas climbed
the chair beside me in his bare feet, his pink-tinged urine
making soup of my leftovers. With my eyes locked on yours,
I watched you keep eating. So I lifted my fork
to my open mouth, jello quivering green
against the tines, and while I trusted you and chewed

on nothing, he leapt into the arms of the night nurse
and bit open the side of her face. You had been there

longer, knew the ropes, how to take the sugar-coated pill
and slip it into the side pocket in your mouth, pretend
to swallow it down in drwosy gulps while
the white-frocked nurse eyed the clockface above our heads.
You tapped messages into the wall while I wept, struggling
to remember the code, snuck in after bedcount
with cigarettes, blew the blue smoke through the barred windows.
We traded stories, our military fathers:
yours locking you in a closet for the days it took
to chew ribbons of flesh from your fingers, a coat
pulled over your head; mine, who worked
his ringed fingers inside me while the house
slept, my face pressed to the pillow, my fists
knotted into the sheets. Some nights

I can't eat. The dining room fills
with their chatter, my hand stuffed with the glint
of a fork and the safety of butter knives
quiet at the sides of our plates. If I could write you now,
I'd tell you I wonder how long I can go on with this careful
pouring of the wine from the bottle, straining to catch it
in the fragile glass. Tearing open my bread, I see

the scar, stitches laced up the root of your arm, the flesh messy
where you grabbed at it with the broken glass of an ashtray.
That was the third time. And later you laughed
when they twisted you into the white strapped jacket
demanding you vomit the pills. I imagined you
in the harsh light of a bare bulb where you took
the needle without flinching, retched
when the ipecac hit you, your body shelved over
the toilet and no one to hold the hair
from your face. I don't know

where your hands are now, the fingers that filled my mouth
those nights you tongued me open in the broken light
that fell through chicken-wired windows. The intern
found us and wrenched us apart, the half-moon of your breast
exposed as you spit on him. "Now you're going to get it,"

he hissed through his teeth and you screamed, "Get what?"
As if there was anything anyone could give you.
If I could write you now, I'd tell you

I still see your face, bone-white as my china
above the black velvet cape you wore to my wedding
twelve years ago, the hem of your black crepe skirt
brushing up the dirty rice in swirls
as you swept down the reception line to kiss me.
"Now you're going to get it," you whispered,
cupping my cheek in your hand.

Melissa Capers

REMEMBERING

I am a sexual abuse survivor on the edge of remembering. It's an odd place to be.

Of those of you still reading, there is a group that flinched and looked away, as if out the Greyhound window at the countryside. You wish you'd taken your seat somewhere else, that you'd never picked these pages up, or said hello. You wish I'd change the subject, or that you could figure out a way to make my voice a part of the landscape: the things I will say as inconsequential and quickly fading as the shrubs, the barns, the houses whipping by. Some set of etiquette might keep you in your seat, wishing for distraction, for an excuse to get away.

Another group perked up: the reaction nearly visceral. Strings in your body, fallen loose through time and quiet (a minute's long enough to slip into forgetfulness), just got yanked. Soft spots just got poked, and you are suddenly awake. You're reading faster, searching for [???] yourself in here. You are survivors, too.

You make me nervous.

My pain may not be worse than yours, but it is not generic. Don't think that you know how I feel. Don't put me in your crowds. These injuries are mine, and mine are the ways I remember. If this is what I've got, I'll fight for it, and all your sobbing for a broken sisterhood won't make me even pause.

Others of you twitch—and don't know why. There's a place for this inside you. A spot for stories of the raped girls, for the girls whose daddies did it to them. Sometimes you look around in there and wonder at the growing population. You're forming your own sorority, a club to keep you company when you recall what happened. I suggest you stop this reading now. I suggest you close each book that prickles up your neck hairs from now on. You will remember in due time, and you'll remember longer, deeper, harder than you're forgetting now.

Remembering for me is like watching a TV with a short—the scenes are all in black and white and I forget to notice all I'm missing, until suddenly the television blazes into color. Unfortunately, it also switches channels—to those ghastly horror movies that I would never watch because the knowledge I was safe would not keep my heart from pounding.

The color's awfully nice, though.

I remember my first dreaming memory. I came to sitting up, the three a.m. silence echoing with my scream. I never knew how much light there was at three a.m., how wide my pupils grew to see. I heard the crickets, and the April smells came sifting through my screens. I was more awake than I had ever gotten so fast before. I knew immediately where I was, and that there was no one home, and I was glad. I was glad they didn't hear me scream and glad to have the moment to myself.

I held it to myself: its suddenness, the huge open quiet afterward, the completeness of the vision that so woke me. I have never dreamed so clear before. I can still, years later, see the bed, the window, see the hand beside me. I can see the afternoon sunlight slanting through the dust. I can feel the terror rise—the terror and the recognition.

I can't see a face. I can't remember where the room is. I can measure the size of me against that bed, and figure I was six or seven. But I don't know for sure. The channel switches back to black and white, the edges of the dream fade off, like all dreams do.

I can appreciate the perfect crime. I respect the one who makes a movie too frightening for me to see. I am in awe of the complete, and so I have to love those memories—those fragmentary bits of fervent color that disembodied rise from me and blaze a path of recall miles wide, years deep. They are, each fragment, full.

Sexual abuse is sloppy. Always. The act, whichever it may be, leaves fingerprints that one day bloom like roses all across the victim's body.

I live with someone else inside me. A shadow creature, haunting me for years. She is the rememberer. The one who mined my body, planting triggers all across me that I or someone else will one day trip.

Right now, I'd simply like the map, so I could plan the detonations. Instead, I stumble into them. The distraction in the shower, that quickly swells to horror as I recognize the ancient, phantom pain between my legs. Silent, sudden sobs that crash like waves across me in a doctor's office. The doctor thought she'd hurt me.

It took too long to learn to speak again and tell her it was someone else.

It's like being in the ocean, or in the wind before a thunderstorm. There's no way to really feel it. You feel your toes lift off the ocean floor. You feel the scrape and bump as you touch down again. You feel your own hair beat against your face, your muscles lift away from bone to tense and hold you still. You don't really feel the wave, the wind. You feel your response.

It feels pretty dumb when there's no ocean there, no dark grey storm front blowing in. I sleep alone a lot now, hoping for the dreams: they're easier. If I'm awake, and up, and meet my lover in the darkened hall, I cannot stop the fear. I scream, and sob, and it's become an odd and painful joke. "What do the neighbors think?" What can "we" think, who live with terror ripping through our nights?

Eventually it passes. Sometimes there's a clue, a scrap of feeling or of vision I can hold until another puzzle piece floats up.

It's hard.

It's reliving once again, on a slow and grinding schedule, the chaos of abuse. There's no timing, no control. It doesn't matter if I hope it to speed up and get it all over with, or if I wish it to leave me alone for a long, long while. The memories come when they will.

There are memories I didn't know I didn't have. "Where did you sleep that year when you were five?" I don't know.

There are memories I've always had, and didn't know to name. Sometimes it feels like my fault, for missing them. The conversation with a friend: "I never liked the way, when I was ten, the doctor used to..." And my friend stiffens, looks away, and I trail off. And then there's too much silence, and she says, "I think your doctor was giving himself a thrill" and I say, "huh."

Childhood sexual abuse makes one, like Calamity Jane, unbelievably ill-starred. It's why so many aren't believed. But news of opportunity moves fast: parents, siblings, doctors, kids next door. They smell the fear or sight the skewed reality. And the victim, like a headless running chicken, doesn't know what's happening.

You remember in the way you thought it then. At three, I thought the turn into the utility room was a game, a mistake to make me laugh. I thought the stranger in there with me funny, then a little scary. He said he was going to give me a bath. Instead he did something that tore the sky apart. He took my body where it couldn't go, and so it went into the sky until the fabric of the sky tore—and all the stars fell down.

Each bit I heal resonates with injuries I hadn't recognized. When the television switches into color, I wonder at the colors I've already missed. I have been robbed of big chunks of the past, and there's no way to guarantee the future without measuring these holes. It's odd—holding sorrow dear like that. Mixing dread with eagerness—and just waiting.

Patricia L. Nichol

A GOOD LITTLE GIRL

When I was a very young child, my parents took me to church, and the minister commented on how quiet I was, what a good little girl.

When I was a child witness to violence and when I was abandoned, I kept quiet. I was a good little girl.

When my father molested me, I kept very, very quiet, so quiet that I did not hear my own voice, my own thoughts. I stilled my memory.

When I lost hope as a child, I never told anyone. In fact, the pain was such that I never told myself. As usual, I was a good little girl.

Inevitably, I have been a good little girl no matter what my age was.

I fulfilled the role so well that I struggled for twenty-two years to keep a difficult marriage going.

I selected a career that was expedient and did not reflect who I was. I worked at that career in order to support my family, not honor myself.

I allowed friends to mistreat me.

I swallowed my anger and my pride because I didn't know any better. I tried to manage the world sideways instead of my own life directly. I seldom expressed myself straight forwardly, because it felt as if I were challenging others and that did not feel like good little girl behavior.

In short, I was a people pleaser.

I was trained to be a people pleaser because I was a girl, because I was born in 1940, when there was little cultural validation for being self-directed, and because I grew up in an alcoholic, incestuous family.

I was trained to keep my feelings to myself.

I was trained to keep my focus on other people.

I was trained to be good.

Unfortunately, such goodness had nothing to do with authenticity and autonomy.

I learned well indeed to be an inauthentic, invisible, other-directed child. I carried those lessons into adulthood.

Now, I look back over fifty-four years of living, and I am very tired of being a good little girl. I am outraged that I learned so well incest's major lesson: to be an object, not a human being. When you are an object, nothing about you matters. You learn to live out a role rather than carve out an identity which empowers you to speak your anguish and your joy. I lived out my role, good little girl, and my anguish and my joy remained buried.

I now reclaim them: anguish at my unbearable childhood and joy at being alive.

I carve out my identity.

I am no longer a good little girl.

In fact, I am no longer a little girl. When I look in the mirror, I see before me the woman I have become.

Rachel Loden

THE PRISONER

Under the floorboards
an eagle's trapped,
its great wings
beat and beat.

Or it is a child tied to a bed, no
many children, gagged
with bedclothes,
I tell you
they are being beaten
down there, listen!

Wind in the trees.
(It was not) only
wind in the trees.
Sleepdust is a drug
she sprinkles as she goes.
Her steps recede. You hear
again the urgent
hoofbeats of your
nightmares.

Donna Hilbert

THIS GUN IS REAL

I have seen my face in the black metal
felt the heat
breathed gray dust hanging
in the air.

This kid knows
what makes Saturday night special.

I open the flue
hide the gun in the chimney.

I am talking about terror.

Now I look for the knife.
This knife is real.
I have seen it at work
slicing the Sunday roast.

I slide the knife
into the shoe box
replace the lid.

Now it's the middle of the night.
I am lying on the floor.
From the light under my door
two voices.

He says, "I'm taking the kid."
She says, "I'll do anything."

Something black comes up from my stomach
covers me.
This child knows
how to die.

Sundays he sleeps late.
We get up early.
I bring her the knife.

She starts dinner.

His favorite
pot roast sliced thin
pearly white onions
potatoes steamed in their pink jackets
leftovers all week.

Anne Stilwell

THE MANY MANY THINGS

This is what it's like now, the girl body locked inside the woman body, breasts a cage, cunt a dark rip in the earth where I fall and fall. This is what it's like to carry around a battle that goes on being fought even when there are no more soldiers, only the ghosts of soldiers and their many demons. This is what it's like when the demons spill out, rise from the cracks in the earth and from invisible seams where my body was once broken and then silently sealed itself back up. This is me with all of my devils, my dark angels, carrying the weight of my anger, my anger like one long scream that unwinds, a ribbon of blood that unravels until I come undone. And when I am undone, know that I will murder you as soon as I see you. Once it will be swift—another time I will make small incisions all over your body with a razor blade until you are a tattoo. The words I carve into your skin will kill you, and the words will be RAPIST and FATHER, over and over.

My body is a temple, its walls washed with gold. Its floor is a river, and there is no end to its depths. Its roof is a bird; the span of its wings reach from here to the sun. My body is an altar, flames of a thousand candles lit for all of the angels that surround me. My body is a prayer sung in every one of my cells. HOW DARE YOU misuse this body. You are evil. You are the bad thing. I will murder you a hundred times. I will slit your throat. I will smash your skull.

Even my grief is pure. You have not left any trace of your evil in me—it is cleaned out as I sing the words anger and grief, a litany that hums through my body, a cloud of locusts that destroys everything that was once you. I called them up. My angels called them up. Locusts fill your eyes and mouth. They eat your flesh, clicking and flashing iridescent in a sun grown dark as their bodies cover it. Skin, blood, bone, they devour all. And you are no more. I release all memory of you as bats that fly into the sun where all memory of you burns. The bats return and fold themselves up in my corners.

I cannot see the end of my glittering blackness. It is vast and powerful. Dark raven shape against the sun, black lava threaded with fire. My blood in the deepest place is black. There are no words for this, but my tears speak this language. The patterns of salt left where my tears have dried speak this language. This, forever.

Joan Makepeace

IN MY FATHER'S HOUSE

A Child's Psalm

The lord is my father.
I am his want.
He maketh me lie down in mean raptures.
He seedeth me below with foul waters.
He devoureth my soul.
He leaveth me in huddled helplessness,
in his shame's wake.

Yea, now I walk through dark alleys
like a shadow of death;
I feel like evil,
for he was with me.
His rod and his staff
discomforted me.

He preparest this fable before me:

He is not my enemy;
He is honest, good, and loyal.
My cup overfloweth.

Clearly, goodness and mercy
don't follow me.
All my days pass in fright.

Someone tell me:
Must I dwell
in the house of the lord
forever?

Gary Young

My mother had the flesh burned from her lips; she had the skin peeled from her face. She wanted to look young again. When the scabs fell away, and she couldn't bear the bright, new scars, she poisoned herself. I have so much to tell you, she said later. She said, I left my body. I knew I was dying, and I could see my body there. I floated away from it, down the hall, and through the door into the street. There were people everywhere, she said. It was beautiful. They wanted me to lead a parade. Mother, stop, I said, I was there.

My father would say, you need a memory lesson, and he'd beat us, first me, then my brother. And I do remember, the little scratches on the banister in the upstairs room, the copper lamps and the flame-shaped bulbs, dark knots on the varnished wall; bamboo curtains creaking as the wind pushed through, the taste of salt, and my brother, shaking as he waited his turn. I took my comfort there; I knew where I was, and what was coming. My father once broke his belt against the back of my legs, and when he saw the welts and the drizzle of blood, he began to cry. I was so frightened to see him change like that, not shouting anymore, but on his knees, sobbing, look what I've done.

Alice Crane

NIGHTMARE

Catfish with oversized heads
broiled to the surface
opening and shutting
their enormous jaws
like so many wind-up toys.

From his perch on the dock
the boy tossed
fistfuls of feed
into the black water,
watched black heads snap
in black water
over and again.

And so it is I go over it again,
stirring up the monsters in my pond,
luring them to feed,
tossing them fistful after fistful
of my own flesh.

It is true I watched a real boy
toss the grain.
It is true it happened
at the pond my father built.
It is true those catfish
were the fish my father stocked
to feed us all
if the Depression ever came again.

And again, it comes upon me,
that depression,
lowers its leaden weight
upon my heart,
and I am harvesting those fish,
black monsters of my family's sowing,
the nightmares never stated, never understood.

Peter Cooley

IF I SHOULD DIE BEFORE I WAKE, I PRAY TO GOD MY SOUL TO TAKE

"Never, never, never," Mommy whispers,
"you were never my baby," and I cry
tears of a middle-aged man sucking the breast

Death has left him. Now the dream contracts, splits open:
Daddy and Mommy are cornstalk dolls
such as my daughters have outgrown and I tremble

the girls will come home from high school
to find me playing with my parents, stroking them,
erecting a new version of my childhood,

that memories cease I call up too often:
Daddy caught in the revolving door with a woman
her nipples peeping between his fingers at the Hotel Seahorse

and they revolve again not to be seen
and are taken in by my buddies and me a second time
and when everyone sees everyone I choke the tears down

and I live beyond thirteen to witness Mother,
a woman who puts away a fifth most afternoons
while she does the dusting, pouring herself into it

and collapsing night after night before dinner
we never have except by ourselves and à la carte.
But the dolls are otherwise: they are like puppets,

my favorite toys when I am seven or eight
and find the Brothers Grimm costumes for my hands
by which I can invent the world I pray to God

where dwarves are kindly and multiple and evil
is punished and a grandmother splits out, laughing,
          from a wolf's belly.
Mommy and Daddy, though, are more than dolls on
          other nights:

they are animals, too, baring their fangs, now they are trees
whose leaves burn streets where I grew up, they are smoke,
and the streets themselves I walk down to find myself,

blind streets, black houses, shuttered, to close me out.
They are the eyes of the houses I fall through,
          they are my parents.
Every night the nightmare, come home to what I am.

Frances Driscoll

THE NIGHT DANCE

The daughters in the night dance around them.
The torn-off ring. Thrown. A fallen star
ground under his foot. The face almost
broken, the throat, and the breasts too, her lovely
breasts. All of her everywhere else and everywhere
small. Such a little mother. More like a young bird.
Daughters forming the circle, keeping
her in. Crying. And crying the night words.
No and don't and stop and please. And he slams
out. Breaking lamps, breaking glass, breaking
anything. Daughters not knowing where a father
can go in the dark. Leaving her. Leaving daughters
with an almost broken mother.
The silent between. With the moving
of closets and bedrooms. What to do about meals.
A father, great bent shadow,
who sits staring into the dark. A mother
in the bathroom with the door locked. The sound of running
water and something else. Everyone waking no one knowing
where anyone else is sleeping. No one wanting it
this way. Everyone waiting for something. Noise.
The moving back of clothes. Everyone
knowing where to sleep. The diamond
back from the jeweler. The gold beat back into shape.
Dinner in the dining room and breakfast a busy kitchen.
A woman with her arms around him. Her mouth everywhere
on him. The night broken. The sound of a man
with his hands on a woman. The sound a woman makes
who can not break away. Daughters
climbing again out of their beds to run, to dance,
dance away in the dark.

Holly Lu Conant Rees

SAFETY ZONE

nightly in the musty, baleful
dark, the voices drill through
walls, through the weak
sheet you've clenched
around your head. the few
words you sound out
from the shredding snarl
could not be your name,
but having surely failed
to make peace, you must
be weapon, or to blame.
the animal pitch rasps
against your most tender
places, which you cannot
make hidden. with all
your small, damp body,
you urge quiet,
would annul the slurry
rhythm of bellow
and shriek, even
the hateful rise
and stutter of your
own breath—
but if silence does come,
everything shudders,
just before or after,
the clapping blow,
the headboard slamming
on your wall's other side,
the howl of tires
on slick pavement.
you hold your own hands
for comfort and to keep
them still. lying
wound round
in your undefended
bed, your skin sick,
your chattering heart

large as your chest,
you can't know
what would be worst.
nothing restrains them.
stark awake, in attentive, driven panic, you
are somehow keeping guard:
against the smell of blood
or smoke, the lapse
of sleep, against the hope
of rescue.

Jackie Warren-Moore

FOR THE CHILDREN

This is a poem for the children.

This poem is all that will feed them for the day. This poem is all
that I have to give. I offer it up to the Gods as it slips through
my brown fingers. Offer it up to all the morning
hungry mouths. This
is a poem for the children. The outstretched arms to hug them
through the day. This soft sagging bosom to rest
their heads upon.
This is a poem for the children. The more I say it the bigger
it will
become, the meaning stronger, more nourishing.

For the special boy whose mother beat his penis with her belt,
his passion like blood running down skinny black legs.
This poem is
the balm for his wounds. This poem is all I have to give for the
girl whose braids crisscross her head like rivers, she writes she
fears nothing while her liquid brown eyes run streams
down her soft
cheeks. This poem is for the children. To stuff these words in all
the gaping holes. To water the dried up dreams,
to warm the small
quaking bodies. To staunch the flow of blood, of pain,
of tears,
years too few and empty.

This poem is all I have to give. This poem
is for the children.

FOR PAULA COOPER, THE 18-YEAR-OLD WHO WAITS ON DEATH ROW

Paula of the trembling brown cheeks and silent tears
I see you struggling and stumbling
day leaning into day.
Seasons and years measured by the shadows on the walls
and the final metal clang of lock-up.

Hungry and wanting, you plunged the knife.
Like a sacrificial lamb, did you think her blood would wash
clean the misery of your life?
33 times you twisted and plunged.
Still the freedom did not come.
The pain did not end.
Only the waiting continues.

Waiting for a kind word. Waiting for abuse to end.
Waiting to be wanted. Waiting to be loved. Waiting
for the time there will be no waiting.
Waiting to die convulsing in the electric chair.

Paula of the soft brown cheeks and silent tears,
wishing you laughter and 18-year-old joy.
Wishing you a decision no harder than
what dress to wear to the Prom.

Hungry and wanting.
I see you on streetcorners throughout the country.
The same soft brown
cheeks and silent tears.
I see you in the faces of a generation left waiting.
Like a sacrificial lamb, I see you,
silent silver streaks flowing down baby brown cheeks.
Waiting.

A DEATH WISH FOR UNCLE JOE

Had luck been with me, you would have died ten minutes
before I met you.
Your soft brown eyes and loving touch made me believe
my Father had
come back from the dead. God had realized his mistake and
returned him to me.
You laughed with his laugh — the same spring brook chuckle
and all encompassing hug.

Yours was the first penis I had ever seen.
Pulsing and purple — a demon unzipped,
a drop of fluid at its eye/mouth,
My ten year old mind not knowing if it was weeping or
drooling as it pointed accusingly at me.
"Trust me," you said. "It's all right," speaking with my
Father's voice.
All the wrongness of it whispered in a voice I longed to hear.
If only you hadn't held me with my long dead Father's arms.
If only I hadn't need to be held so badly.
If only I had known it was all right to wish you dead.
If only it hadn't taken me twenty years to voice the shame of it,
to speak of the not-all-rightness.
If only you had died ten minutes before you forcibly entered
my life.

Eva Schlesinger

AN INCEST SURVIVOR IN A HOLOCAUST SURVIVOR FAMILY

When I read Holocaust literature, I not only feel a common bond to the experiences of survivors as they match those of my relatives, I also identify with the feelings as they parallel those I've dealt with as an incest survivor. Four books come to mind: *A Child's War: World War II Through the Eyes of Children* by Kati David (New York: Four Walls Eight Windows, 1989), *Lost in Translation: A Life in a New Language* by Eva Hoffman (New York: E.P. Dutton, 1989), *Double Identity* by Zofia S. Kubar (New York: Hill and Wang, 1989), *And the Violins Stopped Playing* by Alexander Ramati (New York: Franklin Watts, 1986).

Common sentiments expressed in *A Child's War* were that surviving the war made the person much stronger, able to survive any challenge, as well as appreciate the most simple beauties in life since those beauties had been taken away in a concentration camp or in hiding. In the incest survivor community, I've heard people express these feelings—they are much stronger because they endured abuse; surviving the abuse made them into a better person, and if they hadn't had to heal from the abuse they wouldn't have become the artist, writer, dancer they became. "Looking Up," an organization in Maine that provides resources to sexual abuse survivors, has a different outlook. Their literature espouses that survivors are strong in spite of, not because of, the abuse. I heartily agree. We did not need abuse or hardship of any kind to teach us courage, appreciation of life, and confidence. We can obtain such character building through support, unconditional love, encouragement and validation for the expression of our feelings.

I really identified with Eva Hoffman in her autobiography. As an immigrant from Poland she wrote about the difficulties in expressing herself in English when her first language was Polish. She also wrote about her nostalgia for Poland, her desire to be there, and how she felt as an outsider among her American peers. As a first generation American and as an incest survivor, I related to her experiences. Both circumstances made me feel like an outsider to the communities in which I grew up. Though born in the United States, I never felt American. Class difference also contributed to this feeling. While my classmates could afford to throw around money, I always felt we had to save every penny. I could never afford to do the things my peers did, such as take vacations. Hearing about friends' trips made me envious. I lived vicariously through some of their experiences, books, and travel advertisements. Clothes also divided us. I wore a lot of hand-me-downs, and I remember feeling overwhelmed by one friend who owned several pairs of shoes. I could not figure out why she needed several when I made do with one pair.

I think the dynamic of being in a family of Holocaust survivors affected my being an incest survivor. Although I would like to view the experiences separately, the two are interconnected. I utilized my father's nostalgia for Seattle as a net that would catch me from the abuse. Seattle seemed like paradise to me, and I needed a paradise to rescue me from the sexual and emotional abuse I endured in my family. For at least ten years, I wished myself away into life in Seattle, thinking that life there was better than in whatever bad situation I encountered. Similar to Eva Hoffman's experience, the uncomfortable present situation nudged me into a daydream that disconnected me from being grounded in the present. Disconnecting myself from the present also meant that I disconnected myself from me and all that affected the present me.

I felt akin to Eva Hoffman also because expressing myself in English, although my first language, was complicated. The verbal abuse I experienced by my extremely critical mother made oral and written communication difficult for me. Her silencing of my anger and sadness, her invalidation, and manipulation threatened me so much I retreated into not talking since talking had so many repercussions. No matter how I responded I was never good enough nor able to fit the image of me she wanted to develop.

I became an observer. I observed how my classmates spoke because I was afraid anything I would say would be wrong. I observed how characters conversed in young adult novels. As Eva Hoffman wrote, "I'd rather be with it, with the others, right here. But the 'here' we start from is located in a different place and so our departures are different too" (p. 195). I longed to be part of my classmates' community, to have close friends, but I was ostracized for being different. The "here" I experienced was positioned around surviving abuse whereas my classmates thrived in being teenagers. To be "with it" I had to first get to the point my classmates were at, that point of enjoying life to the fullest. I was in a completely different world, having to survive completely different events than those of my classmates.

Zofia S. Kubar, in *Double Identity,* describes this feeling of living in two worlds. As a Jew who chose to disguise herself, her depiction of survival resembles my own now that I have survived and realize how I survived and what I felt:

> Belonging to two worlds meant that I did not belong anywhere, that I existed in painful isolation. I did not succeed in creating a whole person from the various individuals whose roles I played successfully in different circumstances. For a long time two Zofias existed: the one who always smiled in the streets, and the other mourning her losses in solitude. . . . I constantly felt the presence of the two identities, each trying to overwhelm the other. I could not let Zofia Rubenstein prevail. I had to be Zofia Sielczak. It all came down to survival. (p. 169)

There are many similarities between the experiences of Holocaust and incest survivors. The Holocaust demonstrated an intense hatred of any race that was not Aryan. It resulted in the deaths of over six million people. Incest, and any violence that affects women, reflects the misogynistic patriarchy. Hatred of any group silences that group's voice. To rise above that and to reclaim power is to speak out about our experiences. To keep talking, writing, drawing, dancing, and acting our experiences is crucial to exposing the truth, creating justice, and ending the perpetuation of hate crimes. As Roman Mirga's father told him, as written in the book, *And the Violins Stopped Playing,* "You must remember it all and write it down for the world to know, to make sure it will never happen again. And then you'll let the whole world know what can't be imagined. Even if it does learn the truth one day it will try to forget it as soon as possible. So you must live in order to remind it" (pp. 197, 210).

Cheryl A Townsend

KATHY WENT IN TO

see why Lori was
making such a fuss
like she was eating
her pillow or doing
Indian calls when
she opened the door
she saw her father's
hand over Lori's mouth
his eyes shot cold ice
into her like the don't
you tell anybody's before
but she didn't fear him
now and this was her
child her baby so just
as the I can stop you now
fell out of her mouth she
grabbed her son's baseball
bat and ran to the bed he
was trying to get out of
caught him flat-footed
against his head she
screamed This is a penis
to a child This is how it
feels and gave him every
pain he ever gave her
until he lay fetal and
Lori called mommy with
fear

Becky Meyer

A YOUNG GIRL'S PRAYER

As I close my eyes to sleep
I listen for the floorboard's creak.

I know he'll come before I wake
his filthy hands my soul to take.

That I may pray another day
I ask Dear Lord, take him away.

I know it's wrong to wish him dead
so could you keep him from my bed?

Or take me Lord to dwell with you
I'll live in Hell until you do.

Henri Bensussen

EXCEPT AT NIGHT / WE DREAM

We are absent, leaving
Our bodies

We hover above
On the watch

We don't remember that we've lived
Those unspeakable things
Done to us when we were eight
Or five or two
By friends of the family,
Uncles, fathers, older boys

We think we are nothing
We wish we were nothing

Memory draws a blank
Except at night / we dream

And when a man touches us now
We scream

We don't know why

CHOP CHOP

Chop Chop, she did
Chop Chop, she did
Chop Chop, she cut
away my clothes
Chop Chop, she cut
away my books
Chop Chop, she said
because mothers want daughters
Chop Chop, she said
to marry other mothers' sons
Chop Chop, she wiped
away my face
Chop Chop, she said
you have to smile
Chop Chop, she collared
my throat with lace
Chop Chop, she said
don't talk, Chop Chop

DISCOVERIES

The first five years of my life seem a succession of bright days running one into the other. Days filled with discoveries laced with Texas heat and the smell of mesquite and cedar from the wooded hills of Central Texas.

My discoveries were simple ones, but breathtaking for a five-year-old. Like learning I could see almost the entire emerald body of Lake Travis by climbing up to the top of the big live oak tree in our yard. Or that a buzzard can circle endlessly in the heat of day before spiraling down to feed on a dead rattlesnake in the road. I remember discovering that if I floated face down in the lake, my dog, Wiggles, would swim out and pull me back because she thought I was drowning. A favorite discovery was that the gladioli bulbs I helped Mama plant bloomed into wonderful white, yellow, and red flowers as tall as me.

One day I made a discovery that changed the rest of my life. I found the door to my older brother's room closed. Being the curious kid I was, I opened it. Doors were rarely closed in our house, and I wondered what my brother, Bubba, seven years older than me, was doing.

I opened that door to find my older sister, Sissy, (four years older than me) laying across Bubba's bed with her pants around her ankles. Bubba stood over her, his pants and underwear crumpled at his feet. When I opened the door, Bubba jumped back, nearly tripping over his jeans.

"What ya'll doin'?" Even as I asked the question, a little knot began to tighten in my stomach.

Bubba yanked up his jeans, but didn't button them.

"We're playing house, Cassie." His face reddened and he spoke quickly. He glanced over at Sissy, then back to me.

"Wanna play?"

"Okay." As always, I didn't like being left out of anything. But I felt that strange knot in my stomach tighten more.

"Sissy, wait outside." Bubba grabbed Sissy's arm and pulled her off the bed.

Sissy pulled her panties and pedal pushers up. "All right, but hurry up. Cassie, you can't tell nobody, you hear? And if you do, you know what's gonna happen to you." She shoved me toward the bed.

I knew. I had been threatened the whole of my five years by Sissy and Bubba. I had seen Bubba chase after Sissy with scissors or rocks often enough to know his capabilities. And with Sissy in cahoots, well, they might just take me up into the woods and get me lost and leave me there as they so often said they would.

Sissy closed the door behind her. I walked over to the bed and looked up at Bubba.

He took me by the waist and heaved me up onto the edge of the bed. Then he pulled at the elastic on my shorts.

"Bubba, no." All of a sudden I became very afraid.

"Cassie, you wanna play, you got to do what I say. Now, I'm the daddy and you be the mama."

He pushed me back on the bed. I looked up at the ceiling and stared hard. My stomach tightened more as I felt Bubba's bare chest, sweaty and bony, press on top of me. I squirmed when he pulled at my legs, and he gripped my left ankle tight. It hurt, but not as much as when he pushed himself inside me. It was the strangest feeling I had ever felt. Pain, mixed up with a tingling. I started to cry.

Bubba said, "Shut up, now. Just be quiet."

He bounced and pushed, breathing hard. I had never heard him make such funny sounds. I kept staring at the ceiling, not daring to look at him. I thought, "if I look at him, something very bad will happen. Like, maybe the ceiling will fall. Or Mama will come in," though I knew Mama was at a Tupperware party up the hill at the Spring sisters' house. She had taken my baby brother, Rory, with her.

I thought I could keep the ceiling up and make everything still and fine just by staring hard and not looking at Bubba.

It hurt having Bubba push himself inside me, but there was also a strange sensation of pleasure. It almost felt like when I touched myself. It *almost* felt good. But I knew, even without Bubba's and Sissy's threats, this adventure was not one to tell about.

Finally, Bubba gasped and pulled his sweaty body off me. I took my eyes off the ceiling and looked at him just as he tucked his red penis into his underwear and pulled his jeans up.

I started to whimper, then to cry. I didn't know why I was crying.

"Cassie, quit bawling! Now, you go out and play and shut up!" Bubba opened the door and left. I heard the him run across the living room, up the steps into the bathroom. I didn't know where Sissy had gone. The house was quiet.

I climbed down off the bed and pulled up my own panties and shorts. I wished I had not made this discovery. I went outside and sat on my rocking horse. I was sore between my legs. Rocking on the horse wasn't such a good idea after all. I got off my horse and sat down beside it and cried. I cried until I looked up at the sky and noticed storm clouds gathering. I stood up and walked over to Mama's garden. I stuck sticks in the dirt alongside the gladioli stalks so they wouldn't get beaten down in case it rained.

Martin Jude Farawell

HANDS

My father did not teach me to make anything
except myself, small as I was, smaller;
did not guide my hands toward any making,
except once, a carving knife at my wrist,
to make me handless.
I learned from him
the security of corners.

My father never spoke about his childhood,
except with his hands, with his
father's hands, that made him do
the child beggar's dance
for mercy, to the time of words
that sang him small,
too small to ever be loved by anyone,
even his sons, the sons
he would make dance
after anyone's love.

I get no dance floor at my wedding,
only a man with a slow guitar,
but still, whatever floor there was
became dance floor, and only me,
cornered in my fear, not dancing.
How can she stand
all that's left to unmake
of what was made of me?

And when the wedding was over,
he hugged my wife, just drunk enough
to tell her that he loved her,
just loud enough for me to hear
what he could not say—
though now I think
he must have decided
this would be the day—
to me.

My father, I wish I could go back
to kiss your childhood,
and make it better,
kiss your child with the kindness
of this woman kissing me,
or, if not that, that the past
could be something
that only happens once.

But the past keeps happening in my hands
no matter how I ball them up
as if the blows they held could be stilled
if I could hold them hard enough,
or driven out, into the walls, the doors
I drive my hands into,
or driven into me,
better into my body than into my sons.
I will have no sons
made to dance
by these hands I will cut off
before they make anyone dance after anything.

"EVERYTHING I NEEDED TO KNOW I LEARNED IN KINDERGARTEN"

I sit
in the second-to-last seat
in the row
by the windows.
Teacher gives us each
a crayon,
a clean sheet
of construction paper,
says, we begin
with writing
our names.

The children
hunch over,
ignoring everything
but this naming.
I am the only one
no one's shown
my few pieces
of the alphabet.

She walks quietly
to my blank face,
blank paper.
Is kind.
Takes the crayon gently.
Asks my name. I am
the dumbest one in the room.

Emily Robertson

FATHER FIGURE

For my biological father
whom I have never seen

Daddy
since i discovered my fantasy of your
sexual loveliness
it is easier to forgive
for you know not
what you did
your abandonment
at least gave free rein to
my imagination
and because there are no memories i can be
generous with you
i can give you a smile as easy as addiction
and eyes so egyptian
i can give you a poets mind
a laugh so deep
and masculine it invites gratitude
Daddy
i can have you this way
as a fantasy
because
you went away
i can sing you like a spiritual
paint you as masterpiece
and nobody
nobody
has the heart to stop me

◙ Laure-Anne Bosselaar

THE CELLAR

I want my father to stop sending me down there
to fetch his daily gin, and potatoes for supper.
But there's no saying no to him, and no more places
to hide: he's found them all. Outside,
by the kitchen window, the cellar's rusted door
stains my hands as I yank it open, scraping
a branch that keeps on whipping back –
and grabbing me like he does.
Six stairs stop by a second door, with a hasp
and a slit between two thick planks. I press my face to it,
whisper to the bottles and potatoes:
"Go away, I'm coming!" But how can they?
We're all prisoners in this big brick house in Antwerp,
and damned: I'm the *Kapo*: I have no choice,
it's them or me. I kneel in the cellar, pray
to St Anthony: "Guide my hand toward the sick
and dying, don't let me separate families,
don't let me kill a child..." I inch toward the shelves,
shut my eyes — reach. Sometimes I think I hear
a moan, a sob, a sigh, but sometimes it's a child's wail
so exactly like mine I think it comes out of me.
So I quickly put the thing back — forgive me, forgive me.
The worst are the potatoes. I know exactly
where they lived before, rooted deep
in the wild, salted Polders, where lapwings
titter between cattails and winds,
and rows of loam run beyond the horizon.
And here they are now, uprooted, cluttered in crates,
pale arms groping for a wedge of light from the door's slit...

But then, from up there, comes father's call: weary,
irked, the same every time, with the same pitch
and threat after the last consonant in my name.
Deaf with terror, I grab his gin, a few potatoes,
run out, slam the door, slap the hasp,
holding my offerings to father as far as I can
from my body, throwing them on the Formica

in the escape to my room, where I stand panting,
palms pounding my ears so as not to hear
yet another cry for mercy.

THE BUMPER-STICKER

"Yield" says the road-sign, so you do. The bearded man
nods thank-you, and passes. "It's never too late
to have a happy childhood!" reads his bumper-sticker.
You want to stop him, ask if he knows how. No one
waits for you, so you follow: it could be God in that Dodge,
leading you to where you can change the past like worn
tires, or get a quick lube: the old stuff
dripping out murky and dark.

You'd get a new mother first: the pick of the lot—
a bright color, green maybe--with safety features
and a life-long warranty. A good, reliable car,
never running on empty, with lots of room
for the both of you. You'd test-drive head high,
motor humming, gears changing noiselessly,
and never look back at the old jalopy that always
stalled and broke your back every day.

A new father next. He'd slide into
the passenger's seat and teach you the right way
to drive: check the rearview often, stop
holding your foot on the brake fearing
you'll get hit. He'd pull out Technicolor maps,
highlight the safe roads: no dead-ends, no potholes,
a smooth ride, my baby, tell me where you're heading
and I'll show you the way.

    The Dodge signals left. You follow, but
lose him in a tunnel when a sixteen-wheeler reading "Safeway"
passes so close it almost sends you to the wall.

Susan Eisenberg

ANGER GUIDELINES

Yelling *That makes me angry!*
is better than yelling *Shut up!*
but screaming anything even the meanest words
is better than hitting.

But if you must hit
a spanking on the buttocks is
better than a slap across the face
although a slap—quick and quickly over—
is better than locking a child for hours
in a dark closet

which is much better than
ever ever ever
throwing a child down the stairs
bump–e–ty bump–
e–ty bump bump
bump.

Richard Hine

ROBERT'S AFFAIR

It's all right, Robert says, it's not as if he's my father.

He reaches across and touches my back and my hair. I am sitting on the edge of the bed. I have my underwear on again and my T-shirt but I can't see my bra. Robert gets up from the bed and walks around me to the bathroom. I don't look at him. I know he is still naked. He flushes the condom down the toilet and turns on the shower. He says we practice safe sex. That we're responsible adults. We have an understanding, he says. We can keep a secret.

I put on my slippers. My bra is between the sheet and the blanket. My sweat pants are on the floor. I carry these clothes into my bedroom.

There is a mirror on my wardrobe but I do not wish to look at myself. Robert says I am a beautiful woman but I know I am not. I am an ugly schoolgirl with a Luke Perry poster on her wall.

I put on a pair of shorts and some white socks. The shower is still running but I put on my bra without taking off my T-shirt. My sneakers are in the hall, under the stand we hang our coats on. They are getting worn out. Robert keeps offering to buy me a new pair but I tell him that's OK. Mom says I should let Robert buy me things if he wants to. She doesn't understand why I run everywhere when Robert gave me that nice bike for Christmas.

I run ten miles every day except Sunday which is the only full day mom has off work. On school days I usually start my run at four but today I am a little late.

I run the first mile fastest, concentrating on my breathing. I have developed a habit of holding my breath. Even when I run I sometimes catch myself doing it. Once I am sure about my breathing I pay attention to the way my feet hit the sidewalk. This is also important. Someone once told me I had flat feet.

After the first mile or so I slow down slightly. I begin thinking about my story characters. I write stories in my head about a family that has three generations all living in the same house. The family is very rich and very big. There is always a party going on or a wedding. The eldest daughter is about to marry a prince and her sister wants to go to Africa for five years. The grandmother is pleased about the marriage but she does not want the other granddaughter, who is her favorite, to leave for so long. She says she can stay home and still do good things for people.

"But I must go, grandma," says Angelica. It is kind of like a soap opera.

While I run I imagine these characters and situations quite vividly. My stories seem real and dramatic. But I never write them down. Later on, they just seem silly.

I run and I run. One time I just kept running. When I stopped I didn't know where I was. I called mom and she came for me in the car.

I am in the shower when mom gets home. On weeknights one of the first things she does is cook dinner. Because Robert works at night in O'Grady's bar, dinnertime is the only time all three of us can be together. Dinnertime is important to mom. She likes it when we sit down together like family.

Mom likes to say I am always in the shower. One time she asked me why I didn't take baths any more. She told Robert I used to lie in the bath for hours. These days I prefer showers. I like using the detachable shower head. I can point it where I want. I can watch the water drain away. This is something I can't tell my mother.

Before I come down I weigh myself on the bathroom scales. I am eighty-two pounds. This is way too high. My goal is seventy. It is right for me to be seventy pounds because I am fourteen years old. Seventy pounds equals five pounds for every year.

Today mom is cooking spaghetti. I tell her I don't want any. I tell her I am on a new diet and fitness regime like the one used by Mary Decker Slaney. I think this will keep mom happy because Mary Decker Slaney is a runner she admires. Mom says what do you want then. I tell her I will just have juice. She asks if I need her to buy any special foods or vitamins. I tell her no, I don't need anything. Mom starts worrying again that I will get anorexic like Jennifer Morgan who is in the clinic. She seems to think anorexia is a disease that might be contagious. She seems to think I am still friends with Jennifer Morgan.

Robert is standing in the kitchen. He is not leaning on anything or helping mom with the spaghetti. He makes no comment. In the past though he has told me that thin is in. He has told me that my mom could lose a few pounds and still not miss it. But I have also overheard him tell my mom she has a great body for a women her age.

We sit down at the kitchen table. Robert and my mom eat their spaghetti and I sip my juice. Mom asks me how was school. I say it was OK. Because she has nothing better to say, mom repeats what my teachers have told her. I must pay more attention and get better grades or I'll have no chance of going to college. Robert says not to worry, with her looks she won't need college. That is a very sexist remark says mom. Sexist or not, says Robert, it's the way of the world. He winks at me when my mom's not looking.

After dinner, Robert puts on his after shave. Before he leaves he kisses mom on her cheek and me on the top of my head.

At eight o'clock mom and I watch The Simpsons. During the commercial break we both agree that it's not as funny as it used to be.

When the show is over mom switches off the TV. I think she will tell me it's time for homework but she just sits looking at the television and the wallpaper. After a while she looks at me and at her fingers. I say I'll go up and do my homework. Please sit down, she says. She doesn't know if she should tell me this but she doesn't know who else to talk to. She thinks Robert is having an affair. She wouldn't have suspected anything but she found some condoms in his jacket pocket.

I feel I am looking at the two of us from the far side of the room. This is a feeling I have experienced before. It is like watching a play or a movie. Have you asked him about it, says the girl. She has a strange voice. She acts as if she has no interest in the conversation. The girl's mother questions her. But the questions are phrased incorrectly. There is no possibility that the girl can give answers. The girl looks tired and the mother is crying. I don't want to lose him, the mother is saying.

When this conversation is over, I go up to my room. My school books are on the white desk I have had since I was nine, since the Christmas before mom met Robert. I pick up one of the books I am supposed to look at and sit on my bed, leaning against the wall on my pillows. The mirrored door of my wardrobe is slightly open and I can see part of my Luke Perry poster reflected in it.

After a while, I put the book down and get under the covers. I am feeling very tired.

I sleep and I don't wake up until I hear the sound of our car in the driveway. I always wake up when Robert gets home, even though he tries to be quiet. Usually he takes his shoes off as soon as he gets through the door and sneaks around downstairs for a while. Tonight, mom is waiting up for him.

Good evening, she says.

Robert asks mom why she is up so late. She says she could ask him the same question. She says she called the bar at 1:45 and there was no answer. She wants to know where he has been until 3:15.

That was you calling, says Robert. We thought it was Mattie's wife. Robert says he closed the bar at 1:30 but stayed behind for a drink with Mattie and Bill. Mattie didn't want him to answer the phone so they sat and watched it ring.

What about at 2:45, says mom.

It didn't ring again, says Robert. This must be correct because mom doesn't argue.

There is silence for a while. Their voices have been quite loud. With my door open I have heard nearly every word. Now everything is still. I am holding my breath. I don't even want to move my arm because of the sound it will make against the sheet.

Then it begins again. What's going on, my mom asks Robert. He tells her he doesn't know what she means. Who is she, she says, louder than ever.

Robert says there is no one else. Why would he want to jeopardize things. He thought they had a good thing going. Mom tells him it's no use lying. She has found the condoms in his jacket pocket.

Robert laughs. So that's why you're doing this, he says. The condoms are a joke, he says. The joke involves Steve Patterson and his wedding on Saturday.

Come here, says Robert.

In my bedroom I lie awake. Mom and Robert are talking more quietly. Eventually, they come upstairs.

It's not easy bringing up a teenage girl, my mom is saying.

I want to be with you both, says Robert.

Mom goes into the bathroom. I sense Robert standing at my door. I lie still until after I feel him move away. It is a long time before I sleep again.

In the morning, mom is sitting at the kitchen table when I go in to pour myself a glass of low-fat milk. Good morning, she says. She is holding a mug of coffee. She starts chatting to me as I drink my milk. You look lovely, she says as I walk out of the kitchen.

I go upstairs and brush my teeth. As usual at this time, Robert is still sleeping.

When she hears me coming back downstairs, mom comes out into the hall. She smiles up at me. As I put on my jacket and turn for the door she reaches for my arm.

Listen, she whispers. What I was saying last night. About Robert. There's really nothing to worry about. It was just me being silly.

I walk out of the house, heading toward the corner to catch the bus. I look back and mom is standing on the doorstep, holding her hand over her mouth. We look at each other but I am too far away to see the expression on her face. She waves at me then steps back inside and closes the door.

Gayle Lauradunn

TELLING

Sometimes I think I made it up. To try to convince myself that
he didn't hurt me
that mother didn't turn on me, didn't yell to a five-year-old
"How could you let him do that"
or the old man didn't exist, or the old man didn't do it.
I remember my lack of fear, the pleasure, telling
mother.
He could have been 40 or 70. A deaf mute who must have
wanted to experience as much of life as possible.
Being left out of sound.
But, no, he was really just a dirty old man.
I only remember this experience again after many years
and now it won't leave me.
That old man's face haunts me. I see it even with my eyes
shut. I couldn't have made it up.
He was tall and slender, almost thin, and wore khaki work
shirt and pants with a brown belt, wide leather
with a gold buckle. The shirt had seven buttons down
the front, tan buttons.
His hands were large, square with thick hair on the fingers.
His fingers were warm and gentle inside my panties.
His face had deep lines, the flesh was leathery. His thin hair
black.
He hurt me. He wasn't gentle. But, no, mother stops him.
She stops him just as he reaches under my dress. No, she
stops him just as he pulls down my panties.
She grabs his arm, jerks it away. Screams at him. he runs
away. He is back
with his hand between my legs, his fingers digging.
His fingers inside me and I am laughing.
I am daddy's Baby Doll. I am crying. I am pushing against
him. I am running.
Every man I meet has a lined face. Every man I bed has hairy
fingers.
I laugh, cry, with every man. Mother, where are you? No.
This scene is all wrong. It is a hot July afternoon.
The old man sits with my baby brother asleep in his lap. I
am five.

No one else is in the house. The doors and windows open.
    Light is everywhere in my grandparents'
house. He is granddaddy's cousin. He wanders and works
    where he can in his boots,
high topped, laced around his ankles. He is quiet. He grins.
    A Halloween mask. Some teeth
stained with tobacco. Outside, the windmill creaks.
    No. It wasn't a dress.
It was a pinafore with large ruffles on the shoulders. A
    blue pinafore with white eyelet trim
and white buttons. I was five. He motioned me to him,
    pointed to the baby asleep.
He pulled up my dress, put his hand in my panties.
    No. We were outside,
down the hill in the woods behind the house. I followed
    him out into the wavering heat.
I wanted to know his silence. The baby wasn't there. My
    dress was yellow.
It was my panties that were blue. His belt was drawn tight
    around his waist, his pants gathered.
It was there in the dry grass that he did it. Yes, I'm
    sure.
I'm sure. I was wearing a blue and yellow check sunsuit
    and my panties were white. White.

Marjorie Maddox

INCEST

It's a hushed-up secret
whispered only in a blue rush of tears
to plastic-faced GI joes
or rosy-cheeked baby dolls
who vengefully whisper, "Mama."
Or it's a dead cat slumped on your stomach
who resurrects to scratch your eyes
at the most unsuspecting time.
And it belongs to you
though you shove it away
the statistics and reports:
"Poor boy,"
"Poor girl,"
"And they seemed like such a nice family."
Was it hand-picked as a trick-or-treat prank
by a masquerading God?
That's how it feels
though the echo of divine cries
seeps through your window at night.
It's a hushed-up secret,
too big for
seventy times seven forgiveness
and a pat on the back,
too big for that
till you see it for real:
how it cuts like a thorn,
how it splinters like a cross.

Elizabeth Oakley

MOTHER'S DAY

How you watched him turn me, force his tongue in my nine year old mouth as you basked in the warmth of the fire and merlot. And how you left me for weekends with his marine corps son though I cried, begged you not to, his crew cut head telling me to lie down, stop crying, spread my legs. And the Mother's Day when you slapped my face, kicked my ribs, ripped the head off my doll because I gave you your gift too late, after breakfast, you screaming *you worthless shit after all I've done these seven years*. Even now I would forgive the nights from three on that I pressed the cold glass of your bedroom window against my cheek while he beat you, you screaming, I waiting for you to tell me to run next door, call the police, forbidden to run before ordered, forced to listen to your pleas, his fist, the breaking chair. I would forgive how when I was seven you described the nurse's torture as the Boston Strangler forced a broom handle through her vagina, uterus, diaphragm, lungs, her still alive till it reached her throat three hours later. Forgive if now you remembered anything I tell you, could engage in dialogue, but instead you are 3, 6, 12 years old simultaneously, schizophrenic, unable to approach reality. I too have crawled to the edge, felt the lull of falling into numbness, no responsibility to self or child. From this precipice I step aside again, your hand reaching towards me, always reaching to take me beside you.

Christine Donovan

TELEGRAM TO ANYBODY

help
STOP
my family needs help
STOP
is there anyone out there
i'm hurting so bad
STOP
dad drinks and
mom's in bed all day
STOP
i try to take care of them
but i can't do it all by myself
STOP
i'm only eleven
STOP
and my brothers and sister
are younger
STOP
i would tell my teacher
but she don't want to know
STOP
my guidance counselor just
looks at my scuffed up shoes
STOP
the police come and
take my dad away sometimes
STOP
but he always comes back
and nothing ever changes
STOP
who should i tell that
this isn't the way it should be
STOP
hello
is anybody there

STOP
we need help and
i'll be waiting for you
anybody
STOP
END OF MESSAGE

Jennifer Smith-Morris

HOLD YOUR BABIES WHEN THEY CRY

> *This is how to love..., and if this doesn't work there are other ways, and if they don't work don't feel too bad about giving up...*
>
> —Jamaica Kincaid, *Girl*

Pick up your babies when they cry.

Never tell your babies you hate them even if you mean it. Don't tell your babies they're ugly or stupid even if they are. And if your girl baby touches herself don't put her in the closet. Don't pinch your babies on the backs of their hands and make them bleed because they'll scream all the way through the checkout line. If you love your boy baby more than your girl baby don't let it show. When you brush her hair stop pulling if she says it hurts even if there are lots of snarls. Don't hit her if you pull out some hair and her head starts to bleed. Don't laugh when your babies wet their pants at school and don't give one baby a new paint set when the other one is bad. If your girl baby wants to be a dancer don't tell her she's too klutzy or you don't have the money.

Never go drunk to their Christmas concerts and if they're in the school play don't spank them for crying when it's over. Don't tell your boy he's thin if he's not and don't tell your girl she's ugly if she isn't. If your boy burps with his mouth open don't laugh at home and pinch his shoulder in the restaurant. When your girl asks how old she has to be to wear a bra don't buy a book about sex. If your boy is still wetting the bed take him to the doctor.

Never tell your babies they were your only mistakes.

When your boy wants to go out for football don't tell him he can't because of his asthma. If you buy your girl a pair of pants at K-Mart and they're too small, don't make her wear them. If your girl comes home from a school dance feeling happy and confident don't tell her she's a slut. Don't say dancing is evil and only whores do it. If your kids are loud don't ask them if they want their dad to fall off the whey evaporator and die because he didn't get enough sleep. When you drink too much tequila and throw up on the porch don't leave it for your babies to step through; don't blame it on the dog.

Don't ignore your son when he comes home stoned or when he hides bottles of Mad Dog under his mattress. If your daughter has a boyfriend don't tell her she's flaunting herself when she dresses up to see him. Don't call her Miss Pretty Face. When your daughter calls your son a fucker don't hit her with a wooden spoon and when your son calls your daughter a whore don't pretend you didn't hear it. Don't let your children beat each other up. If your husband works three jobs and the electricity still gets turned off don't say it's because your kids took too many baths.

Never tell your babies you're a failure. Don't lie when your daughter asks if you're still drinking and don't say you've started a new diet if you haven't. Don't make your husband find a job for your son at the cheese factory. If your son gets fired for flunking a piss test don't go pick him up and spend the rest of the day calling help wanted ads for him. When your daughter gives herself an abortion don't tell her you would have done the same thing. If you pay for the surgery to get the wire out, don't remind her every time she makes you mad. Don't say no if she asks you to attend family counseling.

If your girl is crying because her lamb was sold at the auction don't tell her to stop. Don't tell her she's embarrassing herself crying in front of all those people. When your son can't pay the rent don't pay it for him and when he starts having coke-induced seizures don't rush him to the doctor and say it must be epilepsy.

Don't be drunk when your daughter calls home from college. Don't tell your children that all you ever wanted was to be perfect and it worked until you had them. If you never wanted kids and knew all along you would grow to resent them, don't say so. Don't tell your daughter you only wanted one child, a son for your husband. When you throw buttermilk
on your girl's shirt don't call the cops when she hits you in the eye.

When your husband goes two or three days without sleeping don't say it wouldn't be worth it for you to get a job. Don't say it would put us in a higher tax bracket and you would only make thirteen cents an hour or that you don't have the clothes or a car that works.

Don't make your babies pin you down and sit on your stomach until you say you love them.

If you don't like talking about sex don't say only whores do it and good people only do it to have babies. Don't say it's boring and it stinks. When your daughter comes to your bedroom and tells you she's swallowed a bottle of Demerol don't make her puke then fix her Top Ramen. Don't say she's going through a phase and trying to get attention. Don't buy alcohol for your children and let them drive off with it.

Don't threaten to put them in foster homes or leave them and move back to San Diego. When your son moves in with a woman your age, don't say she's a cunt. If you don't approve of her and her two children, then don't pretend to. If your daughter gets married don't say her new nephews are ugly or that her mother-in-law's dress was gaudy. When your daughter has your grandchild don't tell her breastfeeding is for cows. Don't say you held your babies and read them books while doing the dishes.

Never come drunk to the intensive care nursery. When your son is wasted at Thanksgiving dinner don't pretend everything's fine; if you don't smoke then don't let him smoke in the house when your grandbaby is there. Don't tell your daughter you must have done a fine job to turn out such great kids. Don't say the real reason you never cleaned the house was so your children would learn how to do it.

If your husband has a heart attack don't call your daughter and say you're going to lose the house if he can't work. When he dies don't tell your son you're going to commit suicide. Don't get drunk and watch soap operas and keep the curtains drawn. When your daughter says she's concerned about your health don't tell her it's none of her business. Don't promise to see a doctor and then not go. If you don't take care of yourself don't expect your son to do it when your money is gone. If you use a cane and need help taking a bath don't send away the girl your babies hired for you. When you can't stand up long enough to vacuum don't say no if your daughter offers to do it.

If your babies come and visit for the holidays don't tell them no one loves you. Don't refuse to talk about your husband even if it's hard.

When your daughter puts you in a nursing home don't tell her you'd rather be shot in the head. If you have cirrhosis of the liver don't say it's hereditary. When your son comes to visit don't say this is all the thanks you get after being a slave all your life. Don't say you were a slave to your children. If you're on oxygen and don't eat anything but Sustecal, don't lie there and cry. If you're dying and your children come and stand by your bed, if you know it's them, don't be sad. When you try to talk but your lips are too dry, don't try to say you're sorry. If you can lift your arms, hold your babies when they cry.

Molly Fisk

VETERANS

for Dorianne

Our fathers padded down separate halls
in different years, to find us. She shifts
in her chair when I say I couldn't help it:
that's what bodies are made for. I didn't
want to, but I came. I was four, then eight,
twelve—I didn't know how to stop him.

We are reminiscing in her backyard
like army buddies from boot camp shipped
to different fronts of the same long war.
We didn't come home in trash bags—

we are here, under the fruit trees, nominally
whole—no wheel chairs, no bourbon bottles
under the bed; we carry scars invisible
to the untrained eye.

Our eyes are honed like lasers, they're the eyes
of hunted animals gleaming in the dark,
ciphering through choked air
across a kitchen table, measuring
the danger in every quiet sound.

For her it wasn't arousing, she waited
for him to be done. Once her body took off
on its own, responding—she wrestled herself
to a standstill, right at the edge of the world.

I got addicted to the feeling, made myself
come every day of my childhood. She says
her boyfriend taught her, at eighteen,
on the phone. We laugh at that—
with a pillow? On the phone?

Her dog barks. We come back
to what we live with now. I've given up—
at thirty-six I sleep alone, ignore

the breasts he fondled, the hips
I had to watch him lift in his broad hands.
My body shudders close to men,
holding down the scream.

She has gone the other way. Her coming
is a kind of armor—she's piling up sensation
the way I gather distance, still trying to build
a rampart against those indelible nights

we carry in our shuttered hearts like glass.

DAUGHTERS

I am looking over my grandfather's plaid shoulder
examining the molding of a door frame
inch by creamy white inch. The door
is ajar—he forgot to close it
all the way when he came in.

I am using a trick my father taught me:
to get through bouts of nausea on long
car trips he told me to watch the horizon.
I used that technique when he came for me, later
latched my eyes to a spot out the window—
sometimes the Alcatraz light—and tried to block
sensation out: smell of his skin, deep voice
humming, the thump
of his body against me.

Two-thirds of a face appears in the door, brown hair
curls around it, summer green dress, no shoes.
I am looking directly at my mother.
Grandpa's pipe hand is over my mouth, I gag
on the smell of Holiday tobacco.
The whispering noise of his corduroy pants
against the chair is only birch trees
in the wind. She is frozen, lips
half-drawn back, as if about to speak.

Her eyes are glazed, not looking
into mine. She turns her head slowly
the way an old dog will, stupid with sleep,
and walks out of the frame.

MERCY

Tell me it never happened,
tell me there was no deafening
noise of water, machinery,
no teen-aged girl, spread open
on a table. No one turned my head
to face it, held me still and didn't speak.
There wasn't an axe and it wasn't swung
into the hollow air above us, her arm
didn't split at the shoulder, spin
when it hit the dirt, hosing red.
Tell me I didn't see how many tries
before her leg gave up its socket,
how their footsteps made designs
in the blood. I didn't watch her head fall
and roll like a lopsided ball, her face finally
covered with hair. I wasn't there.
Maybe a cloud of sheep blown back
along the farthest hill. Rasp of crickets.
Twilight. Corn in solemn rows. Buckled
miles of two-lane snaking past a spent barn,
narrowing, leaving. You can be sure of kindness
in some other country, perhaps they wish
on candles, lap sugar off their forks.
I was never lifted onto the table,
sticky and covered with flies.
Nobody handed me part of her warm heart,
whispered *happy birthday*, opened
my jaws with a stick and shoved it down.

Lynn Gerber

THE WAITING ROOM

When I hear the knob turn
click of latch releasing
an internal quake
makes my heart flutter
like a trapped bat

There's an instant
of recognition
in panic's weekly
repetition

A whisper of awareness
then the event falls
through memory's
slippery fingers

I always busy myself
read write edit
or terror rises
before the door knob
jolts me

Yet I'm always thirsty
to see him
am quenched
by the safety
inside the womb-walls
of his office

Tonight
lying in bed
I hear distant echoes
of a knob turning
Father opening
my bedroom door
and entering

I always sleep
ears perked to the wind

Barrie Gellis

DON'T MARRY AN ABUSED CHILD

1

i know i am tired
because my face is dripping
onto the keyboard

i know i am tired
because i hate anything
and everything
that resembles an excuse
to take any other action
than to sit right here
and complain
and wish
and hope that i'll wake up
tomorrow
to a different wife

i want to mold my wife
into a smiling
frankenstein
taking parts of my experience
and molding it to her strengths

take my advice, buddy,
you on the subway,
you with the hat,
you sneaking thru the turnstiles...
don't marry an abused child
they are slow to recover
they are not adults
they are not children
they are not living
they are not dead

the present
is simply
a prop
with which

to repeat
the past

you are simply
an actor
playing your role
in her flowering
nightmare

it doesn't matter
what lines you speak,
or how sincere you are...

the pain of abuse
is a good teacher
to a little child
and she knows
how to fight back
against anything
that threatens her world...

like reality
like the world
like papa

2

my eyes are popcorn
and my hands are rocket ships

my cheeks are graveyards
and my arms are guided missiles

my shoulders are boulders
and my heart is a broken pyramid

can't a guardian angel come and take me away?

3

one step away
lurks
destruction

i can never rest
no matter how much i sleep
how can i rest
with my feet in the molten movement
of an earthquaking
volcano?

very funny to you
mr. ice cream man
and evangelical hobo

4

i want to kill my wife's father
who sexually abused her
since she was an infant
and threw her against the wall
whenever he felt like it
and i want to kill her mother
who took drugs and was out to lunch
for most of the troubled years

i want to kill
my wife's
parents
because
they are
killing
me

5

my wife sleeps in the sleeping bag of her nightmares
she milks the pain of her past
like a slave maiden
i want to divide my life in half
and kill the other side,
i want to execute and erase
all those parts
that hurt

i am tired
of being alive
for thirty thousand years
without a break

but i don't want death
as an alternative
i just want
change

Moira Magneson

WHEN WE LIE LIKE THIS

past trembling —
in the wake of love,
I tremble
as I remember them —
arguments, battles,
sounds at night,
a weather
I couldn't understand:
dishes falling
doors kicked in
the wreck of voices
broadcast through the heater vents.
Sometimes
I'd hear him
gun the engine of the Mustang
and he'd disappear
for days.
With him gone,
she'd chainsmoke
and scratch herself
a spot on the couch.
Once when I was twelve
I watched them in the kitchen
engaged
in the habit of their pornography.
They didn't know
I was there.
He threw a drink
in her face —
Go fuck yourself he said.
Go fuck yourself and burn.
I'd always wondered
why she didn't leave
that evening.
But when I turned twenty-six
I said those same words

back to him.
Go fuck yourself
I screamed,
meaning I wanted none of it,
meaning I'd rather be
a cigarette hole
in someone's shirt,
bile and water
rinsed down a sink,
I'd rather be emptiness.
And while he sobbed downstairs
the way she had sobbed
those years ago,
she came to me,
slapped my face —
Do your want to kill him? she asked.
Is that why you do this?
Yes I lied *I do*
and I understood
at last
how I loved them:
that the gift of love
would always be
the head on a platter
and I would never leave.

Jeff Walt

WHAT I DIDN'T KNOW

In this darkness I see nothing,
know nothing. I did not know
what the word *massage* meant
when he said to do it slow.
Nine years of life hide
like a child inside this child.
He touched through the darkness
the way someone will caress
their own image in a pond
to the place where my breasts should've been.
He swirls his fingers like I am ice cream.
His hardness is like my hardness
only larger
like the handlebars of my bike.
His fingers imprint my face
with the graffiti of wanting.
All the rooms are filled with heavy dreamers,
but they do not dream this.
Massage is the thing! He insists.
That word again. What does it mean?
Kiss it, so I do.

I hear the morning paper hit the porch.
I wonder if they'll report
what I've done, if I'll get the electric chair,
or gas chamber or exile.
Good girl, he says,
as I crush my face into his ribs
like I think his child might.
I pledge allegiance in my head.
The morning grass is wet.
The sun unfurls.
Birds search for breakfast.
The world is awake.
I know this is the beginning
because the world has tilted
on its axis to whisper,
this is who you are.

A GAME CALLED RAPE

In my grandmother's living room
my brother and I played
a game called Rape.
We attacked one another

with clenched fists and elbows,
with a hold called the Claw.
And I see my eight-year-old brother
standing half-naked and red in spots;

underwear torn and loose, thin
legs, knees bent and locked,
small testicles showing
like egg-shaped Easter chocolates.

He threatened to crush my skull
and I said I'd cut off his cock
as he beat me against the wall
like a rug full of dust.

When we could go no farther,
we stood back to view the victims—
two lost children left alone—
panting and wondering what came next.

My cousin caught us;
she said we'd grow up and make
perverted real as Jesus.
Our mother never knew our game.

What I saw and continue to see:
the sexual object of my brother,
flawless, palatable and sweet,
our mimic resurrected,

his head on strangers' bodies
flecked with his freckles.
I am unable to digest his image,
eating entire streets of men.

Bella Mahaya

THE LICK LAYER OF LOVE

Daddy is prepared to do whatever it takes to make me good. I will do things his way. I desire daddy, his white teeth, smile, big hands and hairy knuckles. Mother is here too. She stands aside, afraid to come between the lion and the lamb. My sisters listen, hope it won't happen to them, glad it is me this time.

I get daddy's undivided attention. I will do anything for him. Kiss his cheek. Laugh at his joke. Forget. Say I am wrong, say I am sorry, bad. I don't tell him I am good, wild and wonderful; that I love myself, because I don't know this yet.

Years later, when I am grown, I fantasize about being tied up. I surrender control to this man with hairy hands. He has his way with me and it is this man, this mighty man who is sexier than all others—this man with the power to harm me cause that's what daddy did. Teach me I'm no good, show me how to stuff shame under all my organs where I'll hardly think to look. Teach me how to blame myself, how to ignore what rages through my body, what flares up but doesn't escape, what I bury deep inside me until I am gutless. Quiet, stiff, knotted up, hard to breathe, choking. I need air, space, sky. So I try to fly, jump off a brick wall, get scraped and rescued by mother. Oh this urge to fly! The inside of my shoulder blades whisper: "My wings, these are my wings." I lift off, murmur "Mother, I can fly!" Maybe I'm dreaming, maybe I really do lift out of my small bed into the sky and look down at the neighborhood, happy to be out of the box.

Now I tell myself I won't let another man love me the way daddy did. And yet, there is no other love. It's daddy's love I want and daddy's love I fear. I lock myself up. Don't let my husband in. Take charge of my body.

One day I tape a tiny gold key to the back of a silver owl bookmark. I say there is a mystery locked inside me. The owl's eyes are covered because he cannot see. The key is on his back, my back.

Now, I realize the key fits an iron casket I keep inside my stomach—one which bakes and burns, branded with the family name. I put my back to the page, let my own words peel off the tape, deliver the key to my hands. I pull out the trunk. Fit the key in the lock. Turn it. Lift the latch. Out pops daddy and me, he pulling off his belt, saying "It hurts me more than it does you," me with my soft butt bending over his bed waiting. Black leather rises in the air, a venomous snake ready to bite. His power washes over me. Flames. The Inferno burns. I feel the lick layer of love snap my butt. He doesn't fondle my genitals with his hands. He does it with his eyes. His penis squirms in his pants. He's not used to seeing me this way. Mom does all the changing and bathing. She's locked out of her room right now. It is *his* room. His and mine. We're alone, but mother is part of this game. We're all connected by our private parts. Me with my butt in the air, daddy's air, him taking off his belt, his pants slipping to his hips, mom refusing to have sex with him that night, turning her back in bed, wanting to go to the living room couch, afraid he'll get angry again.

We walk on egg shells for days, careful not to ooze the drama out; not to the neighbors, not to the rest of the family, not to ourselves.

Nita Penfold

IN MY DREAM

I tell my mother that
I didn't make it up, crying
because she doesn't believe me.
My dead brother and I are
in an unknown cement-block shower,
my grandfather watches us
silently behind his pipe,
he wears a red-and-black hunting
jacket and green cap.

In my dreams, I am continually crippled
in a car accident. I see it happen,
feel the crush of the steel, the snap
of my back, but there is no pain.
Sometimes while crippled, I help a woman
in the back of a narrow taxi to deliver
her twins, one whole and beautiful, the other
horribly deformed. Other times, I hide a baby
under a blanket in the lap of my wheelchair
from the terrorists with machine guns
who sweep into the room, praying
the child will not suffocate.

    But sometimes
I sit alone in my wheelchair on a high
walkway overlooking the raging sea, the drop
a comfort before me.

SHE TRIES

to love herself, fingering
the soft wet fold of labia,
the unfamiliar lip of flesh
that tingles as she rubs it.
She keeps repeating that she is
touching herself, she is creating
these sensations of intense heat,
she is in control, capable of taking
care of her own needs, even though
it is tremendous work for her,
caught between pleasure and pain.
But she panics, feels this is just
another form of self-torture,
the wounded child within her writhing
at her own touch, leaving her
sobbing when she comes
for what she cannot remember.

Gail Morse

A RETURN TO CHILDHOOD

I will go back into the darkness,
take off all my clothes, stretch
my unmarked body on the sheeted
bed, and wait for you and for the ecstasy.
You did not have to force me, after all.
For you were right; I need this, even
crave it and must have it: the cold sharp
kiss of knives, the shuddering fainting
heat of blows, and always, yes,
the knowing mouth and hands and penetration.
I need them all, begging animal that I am
and always have been, always will be.
You knew this even when I was a child,
and taught my body to crave this form
of sex as addictive and deadly as heroin,
and now as necessary. I have fought
a futile action, seeking satisfaction
from others' gentle hands and tenderness,
but I return to you, with my ravenous
mouth and its incoherent begging sounds,
with this wild twisting body. My father,
do with me as you will, this meaningless
flesh, made thus to amuse you, or others.
For after all, does it really matter who performs
these particular rites of ecstasy and destruction?

REVENGE FANTASIES

I dream of him in my power,
finally, years too late,
but no matter, it will suffice.

Just a bullet from my gun
piercing his all–too–corruptible flesh,
a few quick strokes from my beautifully sharp blade
across and through his aging skin,
or the just–enough dose of curare in his drink
paralyzing his cruel breath and hands—
all that I need is the opportunity,
    the opening, the chance,
and he would be bleeding, screaming, dying,
and at last, at long and much–belated last,
he would be dead,
    the miserable slime,
    the subhuman monster,
    the killer of kittens,
    the torturer of children,
    the man who hit and hurt and raped me.

Even in my dreams, he does not die enough.

Paul Scott Malone

MY OLD MAN SURELY WAS

When I was nine
my old man surely was
one hell of a guy.

His big knobby hands,
crusty and stained by glue,
carried me like a toy,
pitched me like a ball,
picked me up and moved me
like one of his chairs.

On Saturday nights,
as the radio huffed out
some racy tune,
he'd do the two-step
in the kitchen,
the table pushed aside,
my sister perched
upon his brogans
holding tight.
And me, I'd be up top,
riding those
flannel shoulders,
gripping that curly
uncombed hair,
seeing through tears
my mother's face flash by.

What a sight! she'd cry.

When I was nineteen,
too, my old man

surely was
one hell
of a guy.

His big
knobby hands,
crusty
and stained
by glue,
yellowed by
the cigarette's
dye,
cursed by
and with
the mahogany
hardness
of varnish
and a long
unforgiving
bitter craft,
formed fists
of rage.

And
the
service
got
me
the
hell
away
from
home.

RELIVING THE ULTIMATE BETRAYAL

Ronnie you hurt me badly. My body still feels the burning hard thrusts, spilling my blood between my legs, spread to the width of your body, pinning me to the couch at Cathy and Dave's. I was only eleven years old, for God's sake! No it wasn't for God's sake, it was for Ronnie's sake, for Ronnie's sick pleasure, for sick Ronnie.

Over and over you cornered me, pinned me, raped me as it suited your perverted pleasure. How I was caught in the trap of trusting too much, needing too much, fearing too much, hoping too much that it would all go away and just end. But it didn't end for four years, not until I was fifteen. It didn't stop then either, Ronnie. This writing is evidence of how I carry your brutal attacks in my body and in my soul.

I'm fifty-two years old and cry because of you, go numb because of you, I've been denied the fullness of my sexuality because of you. Then I could only know the pain and the wrongness of your acts upon me. Only now as a middle aged adult, do I begin to know the horrors of your raged out violence on me. You, Ronnie, have marked my soul and body—harmed me—for life. Your rapes on me cannot be undone. I have only learned to live with the results of your actions, achieving so far three-fourths of a life. I don't know if a full one hundred percent life will ever be possible for me, because of you.

You are my brother—I looked up to you as a substitute parent, a perceived source of hope for relief from a destitute life. You betrayed that little girl's trust and hope—you *raped* me, you *raped* me, you *raped* me!

I feel certain you will pay some day for your crimes against me and others. You should pay, it is only right and just that you pay for your crimes. I have forgiven you but I cannot forget your acts. I carry them in my very cells.

You said you were sorry once, when I was still too young to know all the ramifications of your actions. I think you *still don't know*. You are oblivious to the insufferable damage you did to me, mentally, emotionally and physically.

I didn't sleep again last night, my body wouldn't let me; it was reliving the atrocities of rape.

Kathleen Patrick

PERMISSION

If it is all right—
if I may talk to you—
if I may say anything—
if I may talk and say
whatever I please—I will—
please say it's all right—I
need permission—I am
still your child—I am still
your child—I still need permission—
if it's all right to need you—
to say it's all right—to say I need you—to
say anything I want—say that to me—
say whatever you want—say you want me to need you—
say you don't—say whatever you want to—
say you need me—say I am still your child—
I am still your child—
you have my permission.

Crystall Carmen

AN AUTOBIOGRAPHY

How does one set out to write about herself? Does she take the David Copperfield route and state the obvious? Or does she search for some profound statement? I don't really know, so you'll have to bear with me.

I was born on the same day as one of my favorite actors, Charles Boyer. Unlike Charles, I cannot claim a birthplace as interesting as France. I was born in Harrisburg, Pennsylvania. Even though I spent eight years of my life there, I do not consider it my home. Harrisburg is a dull, drab town, filled with dull, drab people. I never liked it even when I lived there. I guess I never really understood it. To love or even like a place, you must understand it and feel part of it. I never felt that way about Harrisburg.

All my life I've been a misfit and a dreamer. I guess that's why I feel so alienated from everybody I've ever met, especially my brothers and sister. All of them are at least ten years older than I am, but that really shouldn't make a difference. We should still love each other, but we can't. We can't even sit in the same room with each other for over ten minutes before we have an argument, sometimes physically. I remember when my mother and I lived in Ames, Iowa, my sister Michele and her husband came to visit. She was pregnant at the time. God, I don't remember what started it, but the next thing I knew, Michele was on top of me, beating the crap out of me. I shouldn't have done it, I know I was wrong, but I kicked her in the stomach to get her off me. Thank God it didn't hurt the babies. That was August of 1987. I was fourteen. Two months later, she had twins.

All of my siblings have lost that simple, childlike sense of wonder and innocence that I have refused to let die. Some of my fondest childhood memories are of sitting in a large closet that my mother allowed me to turn into my own private fantasy land. We were still living in Harrisburg at the time in a not so nice row house on 4th Street, with my mother, Michele and me in one bedroom, sleeping in the same bed, while my brothers, Michael and John, each had his own room. They hated each other so much that they refused to share the same room. Still, they fought, not the normal kinds of fights between brothers, but violent brawls. I can remember more than one occasion when neighbors called the police to break up those fights when Mom wasn't home. I would run to that closet. It was Heaven on Earth for me. I could be anything or anybody, and life was good. There was no violence, just me and my friends, a motley group of stuffed animals, some of which have survived and are watching me as I write this. My closet was a wonderful magical place. Every child should have her own little closet where she can explore and discover life. Every child should have a little place where she can get away from reality.

When I was eight years old, my family minus one (John had just left for the Air Force), went to live with my grandmother, my mother's step-mother. She lived in Plainfield, New Jersey. I remember the day we left Harrisburg. I had a friend. His name was Lee. Lee what? I don't know. I can still remember the sad look on Lee's face when we said good-bye. I never thought about it before, but almost ten years later, I still miss Lee. Maybe sometime in this wide world our paths will cross again.

What expectations we had for life at Grandmoms' and God, how far short reality fell. I was miserable. Grandmom wouldn't let me play with any of the children on the street. She thought they were hoodlums. So, there I was, nine years old with nobody my age to relate to. I remember sitting on the porch in a swing watching the other kids enjoying being kids and envying them. I think that is why I play around so much now. I'm trying to get back moments of my childhood that were stolen from me.

Living with Grandmom taught me a passion I've yet to extinguish, though, the fire of books. There was nothing else for me to do in that lonely place, so I read everything I could get my hands on. And I still do. Steinbeck, Faulkner, and Hemingway are my best friends.

We only stayed at Grandmom's house for a few months. It was obvious that it was not a healthy environment to be living in. Once again, boxes were packed and the moving van was loaded. Mom had found us an apartment in Trenton. There were just three of us now. My sister, Michele, was away at college. Trenton. What a place. It was definitely no place to bring up a child. We had only stayed there a few months, when boxes were packed again, and we were off to a brand new city. New Brunswick this time. 258 Delavan Street. My new, safe home, or so I thought.

The day we moved in, peace was shattered by a succession of gunshots. I'll never forget that day. Quietly sleeping upstairs was my brother, Michael; my mother was at work. Outside, I was innocently walking our dog, Champ, when suddenly all Hell broke loose on our block.

Police cars came swarming down the street and stopped right in front of the two-family house we'd just moved into. I'll never forget the policeman telling me to get down the street because there was a crazy man in the house with a gun. That man was our downstairs neighbor. It turned out that he had shot his sister-in-law, his mother-in-law, and several other people. Then he turned the gun on himself.

One of the saddest sights I've ever seen was my mom down on her knees, trying in vain to scrub the blood stains off the sidewalk. Needless to say, all the time we lived in that apartment, I never felt safe.

But Delavan Street was a mixed blessing for me, as I was finally free to play with all the other kids. I had many friends on that street. All through the summer, we would get up first thing in the morning and play all day. But I got teased a lot. I know all kids go through that, but for me it was extremely painful. Until not long ago, I was short and puny, an easy target for bullies. I got teased a lot for not having a father, a stupid reason to be made fun of. Was it my fault that my parents got divorced not long after I was born? Sometimes, if it's late enough, or I'm in a certain frame of mind, I can still hear those taunting shouts.

It was the fall of 1985 when Mom decided she wanted to go back to school to earn her Master's Degree. it was just the two of us then, the way it's been ever since Michael left to join the Air Force. She picked Iowa State University. Iowa. God, I was frightened about that move. But it was in Iowa that I learned to accept and appreciate the many wonderful kinds of people and things the world had to offer.

Iowa was so different from any place I'd ever lived. I loved it. We stayed there two and a half years, a short but very enlightening time. Mom and I were all set to stay in Ames forever, but that wasn't to be. My sister was having her twins, and I guess it was a lapse into temporary insanity, but Mom decided to move to Philadelphia to help Michele with her newborns. We even agreed to move in with them for a year. We must have been out of our minds. That year was a year of madness. I spent as little time as possible at home. It was (excuse the cliché) Hell on earth.

I had always thought that I mildly disliked my sister, but I realize now that I hate her for that year of Hell, of hearing her call my mother insane and me no good and as crazy as my mother. I hate her for calling my mother a bitch, and I hate her for the uncountable times she knocked my mother to the ground.

I never thought I really had a capacity for violence, but that year I realized that I had the potential to kill. I very nearly killed my sister that year. If it had not been for a friend's intervention, my sister would be dead with a knife buried in her chest, and I would be rotting in a juvenile detention center.

Finally, that year was over, and my mother and I moved. We now have a nice, comfortable apartment in a good section of the city, and long gone are the days of violence and insanity. I now have things to live for. A year and a half ago, my calling came to me, and I now know what I am supposed to do for the rest of my life. I was downtown in a bookstore one day, just browsing. I walked over to the calendars, and mistakenly knocked one down. Bending over to pick it up, I noticed the cover, "Hollywood Legends." I started looking through the pictures in this calendar, and the more I looked, the more fascinated I became with these people, even though I had no idea who they were. I soon found myself at the library, looking up the old movie stars and finding out everything I could about them. Then it dawned on me. This is what I wanted to do with my life. I wanted to act.

Suddenly my whole life fell into place. No longer did I feel so mixed up. I had a reason for being in the universe. I have replaced my little closet with another fantasy world. My room has now become my dream world. Now, my dreams are for the bright lights of Hollywood, and some day becoming an elite member of that group known as the Hollywood legends.

You know what the faces of James Stewart, Cary Grant, Humphrey Bogart, Gary Cooper, Greta Garbo, Fred Astaire, and James Dean say to me from all the walls they hang on?

"Keep trying, kid, and one day you'll make it."

Patricia Rose Gilles

MY MOTHER NEVER

My mother never kissed me,
or held my hand.
My mother never cuddled me in her arms,
or touched my brow in a
gentle caress.
My mother never gave me a
spontaneous hug
or tickled me.

We never shared a secret.
She never sang me a lullaby.
When I went to kiss her good night,
she would turn her head away and say, "Go to bed,"
as if I wasn't there.

We never took a walk
just the two of us or
spoke of special things.
My mother never picked a flower
just for me.
She never played games with me
nor did we ever have a tea party
with my dolls.

My mother never called me
by an endearing name
nor did she express any
affection towards me.
My mother never told me a story or
sang me a song.

She never told me that I was special,
or precious,
or kind,
or good.
My mother never tucked me
in bed at night.

She never waved "good-bye"
as I left for school.
She never soothed my fears
or dried my tears.
My mother never prayed with me
or made me a promise.
My mother never said, "I love you."

Then one day I had a daughter.
I kissed her and hugged her.
I cuddled her and caressed her.
I sang her songs.
I read her stories.
I calmed her fears and
dried her tears.
I brought her surprises and
played with her.
I called her
"precious,"
"lovely,"
"wonderful"!
I tucked her in at night.
I prayed with her.

We share secrets
and affection.
We take walks.
We go on outings.
We pick flowers.
We watch bugs crawl and
explore the world together.
Every day we say,
"I love you!"

I wonder,
what will she be like
when she is a mother?

I brought my daughter
home to my mother.
She took her from my arms
and she held her,

rocked her,
and read her stories.
She sang her songs,
and walked with her.
They played games.
She smiled at me and said,
"You are a good mother."

K. D. Emerson

THE FATHER

Power when he was sleeping. Power when he was awake. Power when he ridiculed her. Power when he put his fist through her.

Standing over him, determining where a heart should be, she realizes he has no idea what she is capable of. She hooks the blanket with the tip of her knife. He does not have a clue. She knows exactly what she can do. She twists the blanket like spaghetti and smiles. My right, his left. That must be his heart. On second thought, maybe his heart was lost on the right. Maybe that was why he never used it. She wants to do a Tarzan yodel and thump her chest. She begins to giggle. Burying her face in the carpet to stifle the sound, she lingers over the feeling of her fingers becoming claws in the tangle of soft pile. She snakes around his perimeter like a reptile drinking in the friction of sand. She is alive. So very fucking alive. If she were to die... She rises above him and begins a well-aimed practice. Her arm going through the motion over and over. Not letting go, just feeling.

There is no fear.

She steps closer and raises the knife. She takes a breath.

There is no fear.

She closes her eyes so that for one moment she can feel. Just feel. There is a window open. The night air like finest hair slides by her skin. Her skin, fine-tuned and aching, rises like a nipple from her body to touch the night. Turning toward the feeling, she opens her eyes. Through a cobwebbed screen, up through the branches of a tree, she sees the Milky Way. There is a cricket somewhere in the house. She smells the open loaf of bread on the kitchen counter and pictures the butter knife laying next to it. "The butter knife led me to the other knife." The whispered rhyme makes her smile. She sees her breath as it leaves her and dissipates with flair into a final curlicue. All it needs is a top hat. "What an odd thought," she whispers to herself as she brings it back to cherish.

Thought without fear.

She looks down on him and begins to hiss a whisper. "Thought without fear...," then realizes it would be wasted on him. She and the night could go on forever. He would always have to turn his back and sleep. Again she turns toward the feeling. She presses herself against the screen of the window and whispers into the night's indigo.

"Thought without fear is imagination alive."

She salutes the powerful expanse of night then dissects the splayed figure with an imaginary cross. She closes the door behind her. She sleeps well. There is a knife under her pillow.

He does not know.

Kennette Harrison Wilkes

DEAR MOTHER, I WANT TO FORGIVE

I want to forgive the beatings, knotty winter limbs
lashed across my legs, your hard voice, cutting
"Don't scream. I'll whip you till you stop."

I could outlast you, my anger could too
after years of turning the other cheek, turning
Bible pages written by men speaking of faith.

You taught me to read, said, "Bad girl, stand in the corner,"
and I saw the rolled newspaper coming fast, the print blurred
the cheek, the other cheek, blood to the right, blood

to the left. There is a book called *Why Bad Things Happen*
to Good People. I want to teach myself to read, forgive
Daddy for petting the cat when I was in the corner.

For years now I have been a hopeful agnostic
put faith on the shelf beside atheism and the dusty Bible
Daddy gave me, waited secretly for mystical experience.

My best friend had had one, felt God hover like a presence
over her trailerhouse and tested him—demanded proof
"If you're there tell me how many fabric squares I've cut."

She actually spoke aloud, her needle threaded and the quilt
tight on the frame while God counted the red and blue and yellow
in three stacks of squares and got it right every time.

She remembers—there were 37 and 74 and 48. I am almost
48, Mama, and you taught me to read before school, and I read
philosophy and biology and psychology and I want to

forgive and learn to read again. My friend said I should
read Tillich's *Shaking the Foundations* and I might
because my only phobia after three years of therapy is

earthquakes. The plank floor shook when you came after me
with your eyes flares, and I stayed scared even after
I came home from college with the degree you always wanted

sat in church and tried not to laugh when the serious choir
sang "Darwin's evolution monkeys ain't no kin to me or mine,"
while comparative vertebrate anatomy sang in my head.

Please don't think I've forsaken prayer for a microscope
or drop to my knees in worship of the double helix
although DNA is a fine thing. It's just that believing

doesn't come any easier than forgiving for me, and I can't
help hoping that God is not answerable to me should I inquire
exactly how many words I have taken to say it's okay—almost.

John Gilgun

MOTHER

Your wrist was stiff and you threw a softball
like a man.
My wrist was as limp as embroidery
and I threw like a girl.
When I lisped in your presence,
you cracked me on the head with your knuckles
and said, "Sissy!"
You could make a muscle
but I could only attempt one.
I was your panty-waist skinny-bolink,
your hipless wonder, your *Jaqueline.*
You swung through the 1940's
in your Persian lamb, so confident,
like Joan Crawford in *Mildred Pierce.*
You wore a slave bracelet on your ankle
but insisted you were no man's slave.
Drunk on rum, you drove the Ford too fast
down the back roads of Reading, Massachusetts,
while I screamed to be let out.
"Only sissies scream like that."
You went out to work as a waitress
leaving your apron and a note for me:
"Thaw out the frozen peas, feed the kids,
do the dishes, tidy up. Love, Mother."
At twelve, I fell in love with my best friend.
You saw, you understood, you made your prediction:
"Life is going to be very hard for you."
But this little faggot fought for you.
When Dadda had you down, that time he broke your nose
so that the blood ran over that Persian lamb
ruining it so that you could never wear it again,
I threw myself at his back, I hung on there,
pulling at his face, screaming
until he threw me off, smashing me
against the kitchen wall.
I did that for you. *Me!* Your sissy son, Jack.

FATHER

Father, you wound me
Here is where again
I experience the shivering shock
at the roots of my teeth
when I am hit in the face
Your raised voice
And here is where you turn again
And here is where you hit
And here is where I cling to the kitchen wall
And here is where I run again, here is where I hide
And here is where it finds me again, that mad alcoholic eye
And here at the end of the hall
here is where I see your twisted face again
And here is where I hit back
Here is where your rimless glasses
Break   Here is where your partial plate
cracks in your mouth   Here is where your lips,
your teeth Here, blood   Here my heart pounds
And here is where you hit again
And here is where I run again
And here is where I hide
And here   here at the end of the hall   here, again

Marion Cohen

IN OUR PROGRESSIVE HOUSEHOLD

My father lounged in the tub
all smug and squashed.
It was supposed to be funny, it was supposed to be cute.
We all had been corralled
into that little room
and there he beached,
a great white whale.
His neck, like a rotten tree trunk
his belly like a slimy desert
and *it* like the fat on lamb chops
or a giant poisonous toadstool
or the leg of one
of my wobbly rubber dolls.
My sister sat on the toilet
and laughed as he suddenly splashed
and our mother smiled by the sink
in nervous satisfaction.

But I wasn't ready yet.
I stayed close to the door
not really looking
my eyes, in fact, raised
maybe even closed.
And I don't remember whether that door was open
don't know how wide the crack
but one hand was near it
and the other was near the knob.
Mostly, I remember that door.
And I put-my-right-hand-out
I put-my-left-hand-out
I was trying to put-
my-whole-self-out
was positioned to turn and flee.

STABLE TALES

By age five she was already nuts about horses.

They had tried to keep her away from the barns, saying,"Honey, you might git kicked," but when it was finally her birthday, she was permitted to sit on the gray Percheron. She did not fall off, and since she walked every day two miles from her house merely to hang around, in the course of July she rode every horse in Seven Oaks Stables except the stallion, Big Prince.

"But I don't like to be called Honey," she said.

The stable hands laughed, and hugged her, tugged at her honey braids, and taught her to trot. In her dreams they were cowboys and Cossacks, cavalry colonels, Arabian sheiks.

Were they only old men gone lame from the track, and boys with corn-tassel hair and the warm smell of manure who dreamed themselves jockeys and hot-rod champs....

No matter. Elmer or Joe or Hank would lift her high to the saddle, hold the reins, once more round the ring, and often keep a hand on her thigh so she wouldn't, they explained, fall off. She begged them to teach her to canter and jump.

"When you git bigger, honey," Joe promised. "Not yet."

Warned to stay out of stalls, between rides she climbed the shaky wooden ladder up to the loft where swallows swooped from nests in the eaves. She wasn't afraid of the spiders who tied up the beams. Wasps investigated but left her alone. She tamed the piebald kittens nested between bales of hay, and brought the mother cats Purina Chow so they wouldn't eat up the mice.

When people who hired or owned horses returned from their hour's worth round the ring or out through the fields, perspiring and swatting at flies, she would bring them a chilled bottle of sarsaparilla, cream soda or real root beer from the ice box. Sometimes she got lifted abroad for the horse's final cooling–off walk, or she climbed on the fence to help the stable hands dry and curry their charges.

In the tack room they let her rub soap on the saddles until the slippery flesh-colored stuff foamed like the cantering stallion. The radio crackled out hillbilly songs, and on a decade of calendars nailed to the walls ladies with silly expressions burst from their glossy dresses. She swore she would never wear lipstick nor grow any breasts.

"I'm going to be a jockey."

"Someday, Honey," Hank argued, "you'll git tired of only a horse between those nice l'il legs."

"Cut that stuff out." And Joe, or Elmer, would throw an empty tobacco packet into the cold iron stove.

One rainy morning in August, as usual she walked from her house past the grove of long–needled pines, Tiger Swamp where orange lilies grew, and the willow tree huge as a house, skirted the green soy bean fields and crossed the corrals to the barns. Since nobody hired a horse in the rain, no one was about. The horses ate the damp sugar cubes she extracted from her slicker pocket, then she scrambled up to the loft.

"Here, kitty kitties, I've brought you breakfast!" She climbed the haystack and slid down the other side. "Mother Cat, Mother Cat, where have you hidden your kittens today?"

"In here, Honey!" called Joe, or Elmer or Hank from somewhere below.

She climbed back down the ladder, her pockets bulging with kibbles for cats. She ran to the tack room fragrant with apples, tobacco and saddle soap, and began to search among dusty horse blankets and saddle pads, as if on an Easter egg hunt.

"Here, kitty, kitties! Where can you be?"

"Here, Honey," whispered Joe,"come kiss this nice pussy cat.... Here, down here, in my lap."

She stared, confused, at the strange unfurred thing.

"It's time for me to go home now for lunch."

"Ain't lunchtime yet." His hands reached for her braids and began to tug. "Jus' come here a moment...and later, if the paddock dries out, I'll teach you to canter.... I'll let you ride on Big Prince. Even — " His voice became hoarse and he was pulling hard on her braids, "I might even teach you to jump."

"Thank you," she answered politely as she jerked her braids free and backed toward the tack room door and out into the rain, crossed the muddy corral studded with jumps, then out to the road, past the huge willow tree and Tiger Swamp and the grove of pines, and though it was pouring, and though the car which stopped on the road was only her next-door neighbor, Mrs. Campbell, she turned down the offer of a lift the rest of the long way home.

Lequita Vance-Watkins

LUNCH BOX

I threw it as far as I could
the second I saw her

and ran
to my guardian
who did not guard me but
I needed to be guarded from
the one whose voice said
if she comes
            run
she will take you away

away was where I wanted to be
but the dark brown voice
commanded inside me
            run

I ran
if I hadn't perhaps she would have delivered me
for a moment
if only for a moment

I had prayed one day she would come
swoop me up
glide me out of my nightmared days

so why did I run
back to the cursing
the ranting for
hours and hours

of it from that voice
that smothered out my life

this time I was not spared not rescued and
sank down in the dark corner to wait it out
watching rise and fall bits of flug
the spiders at play

time dragged past
I was told to go back to school

the teacher had kept my lunch box for me and
the humid Oklahoma hotness had festered all its food

the sandwich and fruit full of maggots
alive and crawling.

Bernice Rendrick

WAKING MY PARENTS

Mother! Father!
Like a child
I rouse you from your graves,
reaching one hand towards
each of you, buried 2000 miles apart
as you were torn in marriage.
This ending is not finished;
your discreet death notices
have suppressed the embarrassing facts.

I do the impossible by mind, standing
on separate parcels of burial ground
acknowledging our family tragedies
cut deep as veins that run in marble.
With the silence of the cemetery
you withheld your voices. giving me the ripped
marriage certificate, your union severed
like the neck of the chicken
that ceased laying, your vows
the splintered stubs of Sunday's wishbone.

Packing in different suitcases
you sold the farm and parted,
Daddy slipping into County Hospital
with dirty hands, his violence
drained down a porcelain sink.
Mama running to the Big City
of lights and stars, her new life spent
with a kitchen crew in a veterans' hospital,
returning at night to bolted doors,
her teaching certificate
mildewing in a warped drawer.

The placid prairie acceptance that goes:
There's no more blame than if
a storm arrives in harvest day—

visits as I bend over your tombs, torn
and exposed as I've never been,
going home to what is left:
a few clippings, the plot numbers
and undertaker's forms, some blurred
snapshots of you both in wedding clothes
now joined and sealed in a manila envelope.

Quinton Hallett

AT EASE

Before he comes,
you are standing behind your chair
at the dining-room table.
The table is set with three places:
one for him, one for your grandmother,
and one for you. It is set the same way
every day with the same silverware,
ice water, orange juice, soft-boiled eggs,
skim milk, coffee. The distance between everything
on the table is always the same.
You stand behind the chair
wondering where your grandmother is.
You stand behind the chair wondering
if the shine on your patent leather shoes
will pass his inspection, if the smocking
on your Liberty print dress is straight,
if the bow on the back of your dress
and the line of your bangs are parallel
to the floor.

Before he comes, when you have checked
everything else you should have done,
you practice your salute. Visoring
your small hand, the size of a maple leaf,
you practice your salute. Careful
to keep your fingers firm like he taught you,
careful about the angle of the hand and arm
with the elbow, the elbow with the upper arm,
that the top of your index finger touches
the exact middle of your eyebrow,
you decide you are ready.

He is your grandfather. He is an army major general.
The two stars on his shoulders are spiked and silver
and in certain lights they look black.
He has bands of striped colored ribbons
tacked to his uniform near the pocket
on his left side. The colors mean he has done

something important. You wish he would give you
a colored ribbon to put over the pocket
on your dress when you have done something important.

As you stand at the table waiting for him
and your grandmother, you wonder
if he will be wearing fewer ribbons
because of what you saw last night.
You wonder if he will not have the stars on his shoulders
or any ribbons on his chest after last night.
What you saw last night was
your grandmother and him in the kitchen.
He was drinking from a bottle of light brown liquid.
You'd seen him drink from it before.
She was stooping to pick up pieces of glass
from a puddle of gravy around a roast on the floor.
She was crying. Her fingers were bleeding.

You hear footsteps. He is coming,
but she is not with him.
He takes his place behind his chair
and you see that he still has both stars
on his shoulders. There are no ribbons
missing from his chest. He takes his place
behind his chair and gives the signal.
You both salute. Then he drops his hand
and so do you, but your body stays rigid.
You don't move, you don't sit. You wonder
where your grandmother is. You don't move,
you don't sit until he gives the next signal,
and the signal: the words, "at ease." You wait
and then he says it. He says the words: "at ease."

Marjorie Power

AFTER YOUR HOSPITAL STAY: TO A SECOND-BORN SON

Your voice, shocked by survival.
Long distance but sounding so close-at-hand
you might stand on this moonlit floor,
telling me: it happened when you were
nine and ten, then you sentenced the memories.
Now they've done their time.
You're pushing fifty.

I want to hold you, to draw
your drinking years and hard-
earned dry ones into a harder embrace.
I want steel arms. Your father *and* brother!
Suns, in the world's gaze. *But what a*
mess you've made of your own life,
that gaze claims.

The night sky follows its routine.
I try a novel, a magazine, darkness.
Sleep holds me at arm's length
while your father rests
in his grave. If only
I could ruin one of them. Your brother's
still around, a cold planet in a fixed orbit.

I never dream about sex,
you said, one Thanksgiving.
Our whole table laughed.

David Starkey

WHAT MY FATHER MUST HAVE BEEN THINKING TWENTY-FOUR YEARS AGO

All I'm going to say is
there's a beehive in my head nights
when I drink too much and twist

my fingers one around the other
until the tips are yellow–white.
My seven–year–old son's arm

is slender as a green snake
and bruised from late–night yanks.
My knuckles sting like the tentacles

of jellyfish. His eyes grow wide.
My fist's as big as a highball glass.
I have a Master's in Engineering,

but I'll tell you, when I'm drunk
education doesn't matter. Nothing
matters: not the cold pillow,

not the fragrant flower box
my wife waters every morning,
the tiny purple blooms of thyme.

Joan Dobbie

YES, IT IS TRUE

that when my daughter was small
I did hit her

I hit her because
she was hanging onto

my knees
she peed in her pants

& she made shit in them
I hit her because

she was always there
always needing something

from me

& I was not always
anywhere

I did not always know
who I was

did not understand
why I was

in the life I was
in, I hit her

because she kept pulling
me back into the world

back out of my head
she made me material

cars wanted to hit her
I had to keep her

back out of the street
I had to make lunch

for her, I had to
make sure that she'd

eat
it was my job, she was

so awfully small
she had to grow up

she was only as tall
as my knees

she was all
I was living for

She had to leave me alone

I loved her too much
I remember

— will never forget —

the look on her face
when I hit her.

THE DESERT & SEA MOTHER

Mountains of rock & sand
tortoises
cling to her chest, snake faces
crane out
toward the children
on bony reptilian
necks that are whips, that are
belts with buckles,
                    hissing
you are bad
            you are bad
leaving welts on the bodies
of her children
who huddle
in the closets
of their guilt
                of their shame
until something like heaven
cracks open, a honey-sweet door
into the sea
of their good, forgiving mother
whose voice
is the ripple
               of wind over water
whose arms are the soft stems
of lilies entwining
their limbs, holding them
under
            her breasts
are the pink meat
of lambs

Suzan Erem

FROM YOUR DAUGHTER, 20 YEARS LATE

You must have felt when every
night a cold breeze crawled on your bare
feet as he slipped out of bed.

Did that chill creep in your thin
bones tucked quietly in flannel
sheets as you dozed off alone?

You slept, as peace, slept easy,
soft. From there I know you couldn't
see the acid in my stare.

You slept! Deaf with pleasant
dreams of pleasant men of
decency. My door shut tight behind him.

I hoped each time that you would
come to chase away this rancid
dream that ached between my sheets.

I knew you couldn't sleep
forever, prayed you'd wake before
he left me crying in my shame.

You must have felt when every
night a cold breeze crawled on my bare
feet as he slipped into bed.

Tamarah Petty Ha

A NONTRIBUTE TO MY ADOPTIVE PARENTS

thank you for giving me the chance to have
a better life in the U.S.
thank you for clothing, feeding and sheltering me
thank you for teaching me the ways of *your* world
thank you for the harsh lessons of life at a very young age
thank you for deciding to take the only thing i had left
of my Korean heritage—my name
thank you adoptive father for teaching me that it is alright to
hit, scream and hurt those that you supposedly love
the most
thank you adoptive mother for teaching me that, for you as a
woman, this behavior was acceptable
thank you for being drunk when i was rushed into E.R.
from a near-fatal drug overdose
thank you adoptive mother for informing me that i was an
adult and that my overdose was my responsibility
thank you adoptive father for the belief that sex is secretive,
dirty and something you do with anyone else *but* your
spouse
thank you for giving me material items to replace the love and
affection you were unable to give
thank you for teaching me that to respect your partner was
wrong; being your partner's best friend was unheard of
thank you for the many late nights i had to navigate on the
way home because you were too drunk to see straight
thank you for teaching me that human life has little value
thank you for teaching me that to grieve is bad, and to do so
in front of others is horrendous
thank you for teaching me to bury all my feelings and be numb
thank you for teaching me that the way to handle problems
is to drink them away
thank you for the example you set: spending every cent
you had and never saving a dime
thank you for not pushing me to be the best that i could be
thank you for refusing to pay my tuition to school so i could
live my adult life comfortably and happily
thank you adoptive father for sharing intimate adult thoughts
and feelings with a child—me

thank you for *not* teaching me how to cope with life
thank you for teaching me that life is not about being happy
    and content; it's just about survival
all of these thank you's have made me what i am today . . .

A Battered Woman!

Donna Longenecker

SEMPER FI

Father we sit mute, motionless
as the nightly news lists the day's casualties.
The compression of silence throbs
in our blushing ears, fear
keeping time in suffocating thuds.

Your dress bayonet clean, glistens
on our living room wall.

"Good night daddy," never cuts
through the barbed muzzle choking
the blood from your heart.
Sandpaper lips pull a kiss across our cheeks.

Accidental drops and spills are
grenades, they pierce the air like shrapnel,
exploding in fine slow–motion arcs.
We are the enemy now, ghosts of the ghosts of children
playing dead to cool heated shards buried in our skin.

Sneaking in through mother's bedroom window, armed
and camouflaged, you impress us with
your ability to kneel for hours without blinking.

Watching you hear the choppers, dance
the toe–popping charade wrapped in concertina
wire, we rat–a–tat–tat right back at you.

Your mouth becomes the room, the deafening hum
of the dark, the cannibalistic teeth of memory
feeding on our swollen tongues.

Susanna J. Sturgis

SUNDAY DINNER

Another Poem about Terrorism

(for C.M.S.)

We come to the table with clean hands.
Our mother's hands are clean, she
has been in the kitchen cooking.
We stand behind our chairs until our mother sits
at her end of the table, opposite our father,
then we sit. I sit next to my mother.
We say grace. *Bless, O Lord, this food to our use*
and us to Thy loving service, for Christ's sake. Amen.
Our father's hands carve the roast.
Our mother's hands serve peas and potatoes.
Our hands pass the plates
and wait poised over knives and forks until
our mother takes the first bite.

My father is a sword thrower. I
am his apprentice. He has a keen eye.
A small dagger whistles past my mother's head and lodges
in the wall.
That will teach you to be wrong.
My father shows me how to place the blades just so
they quiver in the brick and leave no mark.
That will teach you to have any answer at all.
I sit next to my mother.
God gets his way.
God never makes mistakes.
Don't move and you won't get hurt.
I am next to my mother.
The only safe place in the world is behind
the throwing arm of God.

I cover my ears without moving my hands.
The end of the table explodes
a crater at the end of the table.
We take no notice.
Water flows into the crater and sits
a deep deep pool of silent water

at the end of the table. I
sit next to the dark and take
no notice.

God is hurling His sword at the water.
Monsters lurk in the silent pool.

Patricia Monaghan

KNOWING THE BOMB SO WELL

After the nightly news and four martinis
he would calmly begin to draw the inner workings

of the bomb, knowing the explosion was only necessary
to ignite fission and did not itself comprise

the real event; how compartmentalized the bomb
was, how necessary it was to keep separate

the working parts until the moment of impact;
with what care the bomb was timed so that

from the exact moment of release it proceeded
inexorably to detonation. Then there would be

the chance to explain all this to the children,
who sat whining or nodding on the couch.

After a few moments he would quiz them:
What were the names of the elements needed

for destruction? What were the parts of the engine
of doom? The proper names of the bombs dropped

on Nagasaki, Hiroshima? The children began to cry.
They knew release had occurred, the elements

were colliding, impact was inevitable. It was
always a first-strike situation. Always.

W.D. Ehrhart

THE SIMPLE LIVES OF CATS

Cold spring rain drums hollow rhythms
on the windowpanes. Two a.m. The house
so dark and empty even the kittens
lie mesmerized by the echoing patter,
heads raised, ears twitching, eyes wide,
tiny noses sniffing the air for danger.

But the only danger here is me.
Once again I've lost it, temper flaring,
patience at a too-quick end, my daughter
crying, and my wife's heart sinking
in the sadness of another good day gone bad.
If sorry has a name, it must be mine.

The kittens don't suspect a thing.
One turns her head to lick my hand.
The other, having satisfied herself
this new sound filling up the night
is just another harmless curiosity,
stirs once, then settles in my lap.

Tonight my wife and child are sleeping
somewhere else. I've done this to myself
often enough to wonder just how many
chances I've got left. I stroke the cats,
who purr like engines; happy to be near,
they see no need for my improvement.

Karl Elder

DAWN RUN

My dog must've seen another monster,
barking at debris floating in the bloated

river. So had I, last night.
Overhead, a gull's cry is hysterical,

as though belonging to another species,
banded, then abandoned—*ow, owwww.*

By the third mile I hear the owl.
Now geese: insane, incessant honking

in the direction we return
as if my mind is trying to escape

the moment it contains—the last
time, I swear, I've slapped my son.

Nancy Takacs

PONTIAC

My father stumbles down Avenue A,
home again, with his bourbon, crushed poinsettias,
all he couldn't hold,
to disappear into a plate of kielbasa
or kidney stew, then argue
with the woman waiting to blame him,
then the broken eggs,
crying over dessert, the doors,
quietly closing, nightly sounds
with no one to interrupt.

Cut from barfights, confused in the mornings,
at the table, he looked out
at the old peach trees,
the cigarette now lit. The pacing began,
that way he woke up taking the smoke in,
ready for a Saturday of goodness,
then sitting at the front
window, crosswording, jumbling,
the room converted with almanacs,
dictionaries, all open.

If I want to remember why I left that city
I think it was darkness, hardly any parks,
loving the truth as I drove down
our street lined with cars, when he told me
I was going to be like him,
that I was already him, drinking, smoking,
and liking it, running around Bayonne
at midnight with no one.

He with his swollen welder's hands
that shook, who left in the middle of countless
Christmas dinners to get through them,
who sat with me in his Pontiac,

the only new car he ever earned,
and tried to teach me
when I turned the corners to let it slip out
like a boat on Newark Bay. All I felt
were the fins that frightened me
and a wake I left trailing through those narrow streets.

Elizabeth Claman

GOOD-BYE TO THE DUST JACKET SATYR

Thin eyes. Lips tight as a clenched flower,
Daddy—dead now twenty years—
this black and white dust jacket photo
hides your ruddy cheeks and sunblond hair,
your eyes, like chips of winter sky,
though sometimes I remember you, bright
as '50s Technicolor—demon laugh,
and fingers claw my knees and thighs.

For years, I held your secret, saying only
He is so smart, my father.

Bruises, excused.
Dart board daughter.
Razor strop.
Back hand knuckles in my eye.

And yet,
riding your bike through Central Park,
grinning above your chambray shirt,
you seemed the perfect aging boy.

And the stories you told:
Winter storm off Montauk—
lashed to the mast, like Odysseus, you said,
until the Coast Guard found you.
How I thrilled to hear it,
despite
the night when I was 12.
You crawled drunk into my bed,
pressed your cock
to my ass and fell asleep.
Or, later,
cornered me
in elevator or hallway
sliding
your fingers into the damp
between my thighs.

Or watched me dress,
stroking the keloid scar on your belly,
only to swear I was hideous,
eyes like pee holes in the snow,
lank hair, crooked teeth, and *Fat,*
you would say.
Who will ever want you, who?

There are nights, since you died,
I dreamed feeding you to dogs,
the bowl of your skull licked clean.
Or gelding you with a sharp knife.

Though I have shot you at point blank range
and pushed you down stairs,
you have not left me.
These twenty years,
time and again,
I've loved in your image
smart men with heavy hands
who held their hearts high out of reach,
like some game played
with
dog and ball.

But tonight,
Daddy,
twenty years from the day
of your death,
I peel the dust jacket from your book,
touch a match to your face,
watch it curl in the fire.

Your cheek,
eyes,
slash of a smile.

Over the flames,
I whisper your favorite phrase.
Fuck you, I say.

Then sit up late,
sifting your dust jacket ashes,
reading them
        as if for signs.

The smell of your smoke
still sweet in my house,
your dust on my fingers,

one bone at a time,
    I uncurl —
            my back, neck, arms.

I run my breath
over belly, ass, thighs,
          breathing your death fire
          into every cell.

You are beautiful, I say to my face, to my eyes.
Beautiful, to my hair and my teeth.

Then I eat your ashes, Daddy,
licking my fingers, licking them clean.

I wash you down with water and with wine.

When I walk outside,
the night smells of jasmine and pine sap.
Each star a road map.
My mouth is open,
I breathe in and out.

I will eat anything now
          to stay free.

PART II ⊠ FROM MY WINDOW, I SEE MOUNTAINS
THE JOURNEY TOWARD HEALING

Aerodynamically, the bumble bee should not be able to fly, but the bumble bee doesn't know it, so it flies anyway.

—Mary Kay Ash

Love yourself; get outside yourself and take action. Focus on the solution. Be at peace.

—Sioux saying

Gary Young

SLEIGHT OF HAND

I have nothing to hide.
If I seem to conceal
a ball, an egg or a lady's
handkerchief, it is mere

illusion. The trick
is not in making things
disappear, it is
bringing them back.

I begin with a memory.
It is the memory
of my mother. She is
pregnant with my younger brother

although she is thinking
of something else.
I close my hands gently
over her and open them

to reveal the dove, pure white.
This is no simple deceit.
I spread my fingers
and in the spaces between

your uncles are singing
a melody. Your father
is with them, still
singing off key.

This makes you cry. Please,
take this silk handkerchief
and keep pulling;
it is long enough

for all your sorrows.
Your grandmother's death,
your virginity and
the porcelain doll you kept

hidden so long in the closet
are waiting to return.
Even the scar under your chin,
the one you forgot you had,

is part of my act.
A snap of my fingers
and I fill the room
with flowers. Flowers so clever

they bleed. Take this knife
from behind my ear, the
bone-handled one you lost
at the harbor. It is sharp

as ever; cut yourself
a rose. Cut one for each of us.
We are all magicians.
We can have our way.

Molly Fisk

SURRENDER

When the truth came to me,
slipped into my house in its white
robes, its face open as my face,
its heart obvious and trusting,
I stood calmly in the front hall
and did not move to bar the door.

When the truth laid its cool hand
on my sleeve and said,
Come with me, it's time, I went
quietly. She led me into the past,
through the backyards I once
knew, bedrooms and kitchens;
we sat in my father's car and talked.

I was shivering in my thin skin
and crying readily by this time: terrified,
furious. She offered her own consolation—
no false pats on the hand and no shoulder
to lean on, I had to learn to stand upright
or bend on my own. In her clear voice
the truth offered all she has to give us:
Herself, and the stern comfort
of belonging to this world.

Laure-Anne Bosselaar

FROM MY WINDOW, I SEE MOUNTAINS

The morgue man pulls my father out of wall C:
the drawer so heavy he must brace his foot
against another one to pull it open. It jams
half-way, this is how far it will go: one half
available for viewing, the other no.

A voice cries out in the anteroom, then turns
into a wail so unbearable the morgue man leaves.
I'm alone with my father again. This time, I
lift the sheet further than allowed, and look.
This time, it is he who is frozen. And I see his

rage, down there in the dark – like a fist crammed
between his legs. I touch his hands, the huge
Dutch hands that almost killed me, almost killed
my daughter, but once – on a shore in The Hague –
built me a sand castle, the morning after

his mother's funeral. It took him all day,
the deepest terror I remember, watching him
build that castle with the odd tenderness of brutes,
stroking the sand with weightless hands while I
sat at a distance, not knowing what to think,

what to do, Dutch rain sprinkling the sands
like a blessing. When the castle was done, he raised
moats around it, and mountains circling them,
while dusk wrapped us in its cerements, then night.
Not a word was uttered, even when we climbed the dunes

back to his mother's house, where I watched him
rock her wooden shoes in his lap, a hand in each
battered thing, the kitchen stove sighing.
After I buried him next to her, I flew back to this new
country, to this house surrounded by mountains,

with mountains around them. Some days, they seem
so quiet, so immutable I think: shock, fissure, fault;
I think: chasm, quake, wave. But I pray: plant me here
a while longer, plant this in me deep: nothing's perpetual,
eternity only a word – kind as consolation, but as brief.

Claudia Yukman

HALF-HEARTED

Half-heartedly, I lay my hand across the table.
"It takes courage," a stranger says.

Half of my father's heart is dead.
He drowned without it.

My sister the swimmer runs over water.
At a distance I am already pushing at his heart.

Your children, we pull your body
out of the past, onto forgiving sand.

The father is too heavy for the child to carry.
Her breath catches as he stands at the door.

Now in your lost memory you are light
as a child, light as a child carried by a child.

The courage it takes to move the body,
to push gravity back, to fall into the sky

light as laughter, this untried

courage bears the body down.

☒ Allie Light

THREE VERSIONS OF
THE MAN IN THE BASEMENT

1 • Memory and Family Lore

The near total eclipse of the past by the present—that dark sun of memory leaking along the rim of today—sometimes allows me glimpses of the year I was four. I remember in half-light that my brother was in the room, *or* that he was not. The voice on the radio had a silent space between each word. I brought a jar of caterpillars from the bushes outside. The man downstairs rubbed me with something that grew on him. *It* was by the top of his legs and bubbles came out. I was afraid of spiders and moths.

Like radioactive decay, experience remains by half, or again by half in the dimly lit interiors of memory. What I remember fragments and falls into strings like flax. When I was four my mother told me clothes were made from flax. I embroidered with brown thread and two hoops. She tied the thread in a knot.

The man downstairs whispers that he will cut off my head if I tell. In my dream the caterpillars escape, but in the moonlight I see their dark bodies behind the glass. My mother says, "In two weeks it will be your birthday." Every day I say, "In two weeks it's my birthday." Then she says, "No, no, it's tomorrow." I don't understand. Is she fooling me? She laughs and says, "Time passes."

In 1992, 53 years after I was molested, I recorded a conversation with my father, Thurman (who becomes Roy in the novel) when my father was 78 and I was 57:

Allie: *I was molested by the stepfather of Hazel. Would you say how you went to him and what you said to him?*

Thurman: *This friend of Mack Posey that I spoke of had a Luger—a 30 Luger —and he was afraid the FBI might drop in his house and search it sometime and find it and he might be in trouble. So he asked me to keep it for him and we put it on top of the cupboard and so I got that Luger and carried it right in my hands so he could see it and I told him to get out of the area and not come back and I don't remember seeing him after that.*

Allie: *How did you find out?*

Thurman: *Your mother tells me that you were complaining about uh—vaginal itching, or problems of some kind and so your mother said, 'Well, have you had your fingers in there?' And you said, 'No, but Johnny Ayellus has.'*

Allie: *I don't remember that. I remember...it must have been the first time I was molested by him and he didn't touch me in any way except to rub his penis on me until he ejaculated—which was all over the front of me and I was only this small...just all over the front of me. That's the only memory I have. I don't remember that he ever put his hands in my vagina.*

Thurman: *Well it was only recently that your mother told me about that ejaculation bit and that he had a handkerchief and wiped it up...*

Allie: *Yeah, and tied my hair ribbon and put my clothes back on me. I have no idea how many times it happened. I have only the one memory of that one time.*

Thurman: *I've often thought I should have taken that son-of-a-bitch into the basement where there was a brick wall and made him put his hand up on the wall and shot through his hand—but what I did was effective enough that he left.*

Allie: *I'm sure he took his molesting along with him and did it to the next kid he got his hands on, but...*

Thurman: *...he would have in any event.*

Allie: *...but at least he didn't kill me. I mean, I'm grateful for that.* (Long pause) *I'm proud of you that you did that—see I have no memory of the gun. I have the family story which is that you told him he had 24 hours to get out of there or you'd call the police—that's what I always heard. I like the fact* (laughs)*that there was a gun in the house. That will be much more dramatic to write about. I remember him as being very old—like an 80 or 90 year old man.*

Thurman: *No, he was about 30.*

Allie: *That shows you—four and a-half year old kids don't have any idea how old people are.*

Thurman: *I was so angry, it was all I could do to keep from shooting the son-of-a-bitch, but I realized that I would be split up from my family, and my family would suffer a great deal more over it and, after all, in those days his words would have carried as much weight as yours.*

Allie: *But he would have been dead.*

Thurman: *But he would have been dead.*

2 • The Novel

I am thus led to the proposition
that there is no fiction or nonfiction
as we commonly understand the
distinction: there is only narrative.
—E. L. Doctorow

Narrative means the act of telling the story. We writers and filmmakers are storytellers, and whether our work is called fiction or nonfiction, we strive to tell our stories through the invention of dramatic elements and the combination of dissimilar or incongruous incidents. When experience is re-remembered in order to be told, the experience is changed; what's forgotten or left out puts a new spin on memory. When I was re-creating—as a scene in a novel, and then as an episode in a film—the sexual molestation that I experienced at the age of four, I combined several different memories from that period and surrounded those memories with invention. I had remembered, in some detail, the physical act—he placed me on a chair, removed my clothes, rubbed his penis against me and ejaculated on my body. However, I remembered no fear. Since he threatened to cut off my head if I told what he had done, I assumed I would have been frightened. As well as remembering the physical act, I also had clear images of the place: A dank basement room filled with broken furniture. One window at sidewalk level. A dirt floor. In order to create sub-text and texture for the novel's plot, I then took other memories from my childhood and wove those into the molestation incident in order to build the story.

Because written language and film language are distinct mediums, the method of storytelling becomes different for each. In my novel each chapter presents the voice of an individual member of the family. The child, Jane, experiences the molestation and we read it from her point-of-view. The molester is confronted in a chapter written in the voice of the father, Roy. Presented here are parts of two chapters in Jane's voice.

Excerpts from *Blind Man Tapping*, a novel

The blind man could not see. The bathroom had no windows and mama said being blind was like being in a room with no windows in the darkest part of the night. But still there was the moon and the light bulb. What about those? "No moon. No light bulb," mama said. What about when you cover your face and press your fingers into your eye and fire shoots out? "That's not blind," Gin said, "it's your eyeballs screaming 'ouch, ouch'."

The blind man lived downstairs. He waved his stick on the street and it made a steady sound. When Gin wanted Janie and Richie to behave, she made the blindman-stick-sound with her tongue.

Roy said the blind man darted into his house like a troll who lived under a bridge. But this was not a bridge, this was number 17-A Langton. Gin would show Jane how to print her address in case she got lost.

All the children played with the blind man. He was in the circle and they threw things at him. Jane had thrown a tin can. They chanted, "Blind man, blind man, hit me, hit me!" as they dodged and leaped near his stick. The blind man whirled around; once he cried, but usually he swore at them.

"Don't torment him," Gin told her. Jane liked the words the children made up about him.

"He pees in his bed and he shits in his whiskey," they shouted.

One boy sang out, "He fucks his wife with his blind man's stick!"

"Your mothers are all whores," the blind man screamed.

Richie was looking over the balcony next to Hazel's door. He spit down on the blind man in long, silver threads.

Jane giggled as she hopped on and off the curb. "Pees in his bed, pees in his bed," she sang.

Her friend Chacha had a glass jar. "Let's catch caterpillars," she said. They went into the vacant lot and the creatures tickled the insides of their cupped hands. Chacha stepped on one to show Jane its green guts, and she sang a song, "Jeepers, creepers, whered'ja get those weepers? Whered'ja get those eyes?"

"You're boring," Chacha said to Jane, "you're too little." She went off to play with another girl and left the jar on the ground. Jane found a mother and a baby caterpillar and put them inside with the others. "Get into your house, Sir," she said.

Bang, bang. The sound was against the side of the building. She looked up and saw Al hitting the broom out the window. Specks of dirt flew into the air above her head.

"Hi Al," she waved.

He looked over the windowsill. "What are you doing down there?"

"Getting caterpillars," Jane shouted.

"What do you want to do that for?"

"To play with 'em." She lifted her arms and the jar of grasses and sticks shone in the sun.

Jane saw the head of Al come out the back door. It rode down the staircase bannister like a car on a track, until his whole body stood in the doorway leading from their yard into the lot.

"Jane, come here for a minute," he said."Let me see what you caught."

She turned the lid tight on the jar and carried it in both hands to the fence. She noticed that the baby one was climbing the glass, tiny drops of sun wiggling on its individual hairs, brown and black.

Al said she needed holes in the lid so the caterpillars could breathe and they looked for a nail on the basement floor. He pounded the nail with a rock, but it wouldn't go through the tin. Next he tried an empty can. "Jesus Christ," he said, and threw it aside. On the window was an iron without a handle and he hit the nail with that and a hole came in the top.

Jane thought the basement smelled funny, but she could see the outlines of things in the light from the window. Al promised her those were not spider webs, they were cobwebs and cobwebs don't have spiders. The room was full of furniture.

"It's all broken," he said, as he took down a chair that was hanging up high.

"I'll show you another game we can play." And he took the jar from her and set it on the ground. "This is a new game." He lifted her onto the chair. "And with this game you get to have some candy."

Al took off each piece of her clothes until she stood on the chair with out anything. The buttons of his shirt were in front of her eyes. His zipper made a little sound and she saw his wee-wee come out. He rubbed his wee-wee all over her and he sounded like Roy when Roy played with them at the beach, when he dropped down on the sand and said, "No more, I'm winded," and then Roy pretended he couldn't catch his breath. At the top of her legs where she made pee-pee, Al squeezed bubbles on her. She could see feet walking by the window. Al took his handkerchief and wiped all over Jane. He wiped the bubbles from between her legs and off her belly. He tied her hair ribbon.

"When do we get to have the candy?" Jane asked.

Al stirred his hand around in the kitchen cupboard and he gave her two gumdrops. One black and one orange. She climbed the stairs with her jar of caterpillars; she had the orange candy in her mouth and the black candy in her hand.

"Jane," Al said from the bottom of the stairs, "if you tell anyone about our game, I'll cut off your head."

▩ ▩ ▩

Bluebeard's wife's hair grew from Jane's own head and the bleeding ends dripped on her face. Dark blotches of blood fell upon the caterpillars squirming over the pillow and a steady sound was in the room—not the blind man's stick, but the shoes of the wife as she was dragged up the basement stairs. She opened her eyes and it was not blood. Tears were spilled everywhere. Tears were all over the bed. She could see from the light-well that the jar was on the floor, its lid tightly closed. And then the shoe sound stopped.

"You're having a nightmare," Gin whispered, turning on the light. She put her hand on the sheet where all the tears were.

"Why Jane, you've wet the bed!" she said.

"Tomorrow you dump those caterpillars back in the lot," Gin told Jane as she changed the bed. "I'd have nightmares too, if they were the last thing I laid eyes on before I fell asleep." The tears continued to fall from Jane's eyes and Gin decided she'd better stay in the room for a while. At least Roy had finished before Jane woke up and he wasn't waiting on her to come back to bed.

"You want me to sit with you?" she asked. Jane nodded.

Gin shivered in her thin slip. She looked at the child's slight face and wondered why her features were so small. She's on her way to becoming invisible, Gin thought.

"I'll just hop under the covers," she said, sliding in beside Jane. The child was really a bundle of twigs covered with skin. She had forgotten how small, how young Jane was. The oldest one grows up fast she thought, and then she remembered that she, too, was one of those. Jane put her thumb in her mouth and they embraced each other in the narrow bed and slept.

3 • The Film

The two elements considered to be the backbone of nonfiction film are: *Cinéma vérité*—real film—taking the camera into the streets, into the lives of people *and* the on-camera interview. Use of *Cinéma vérité* is one way of creating action in a film, though by no means the only way. *Cinéma vérité* documents what is happening in the present. The interview is always about the past.

My partner Irving Saraf and I have created another component for visualizing the film story—an element that we call the *emotional equivalent*. Our *emotional equivalent* is a direct descendant of the 1929 photographs of clouds by Alfred Stieglitz. He called these pictures of clouds *equivalents* because, he said, they transcended 'literalness'—becoming the *poetic equivalent* of reality. Our *emotional equivalents* are nonliteral, transformative images that describe feelings. They are devices that unlock images from one's inner world, devices to use in the creation of dreams, fantasies, imagination—impossible images to capture with *Cinéma vérité*.

The Molestation Scene From *Dialogues With Madwomen*

When I was re-creating on film the incident of sexual molestation which took place in a basement when I was four years old, I concentrated on three memories from my early childhood: first, the physical act; second, my fear of spiders and the memory that someone (my mother?) had told me that cobwebs were harmless because spiders dwelt in spider webs, not cobwebs; and third, my capturing caterpillars in a vacant lot, which resulted in a nightmare where worm-like monsters escaped the jar and were crawling on my bed.

In order to dramatize these memories I began searching vacant lots and other open spaces for caterpillars. The Woolly Bear Caterpillar of my youth is nearly extinct, but in Berkeley I found some picturesque caterpillars, green as grass with black spots on their bodies, and brought them home. I filmed my partner's hand hammering holes in the jar lid, and closeups of the creatures wriggling inside the glass. During this same time spiders had begun building their yearly magnificent webs on the wooden supports of our deck, so we lit them at night and filmed the spiders at work. Ultimately a choice had to be made between caterpillars and spiders and I felt that for this particular subject, the spider had become the better metaphor.

I combined these memory-images into one sequence. I knew from the beginning that the child would not be shown—the scene would be from her point-of-view and the first shot was to be the man's hand holding the child's hand, their hands and wrists large in the foreground and in the background the dark basement into which he is leading her. We put a piece of plywood on a mover's dolly and converted it to a platform on wheels where the camera person sat and was pushed close behind the two as they walked—thus the basement is revealed from a low, moving position as if through the girl's eyes.

The director must always ask herself, *Who is looking and who is being seen?* Reality is exploited when the camera lingers on the victim. I prefer to see what the victim sees—to view the molester, the room of broken furniture, the people passing freely and unconcerned beyond the window. The *real* window of the *real* basement showed only feet walking past. I had to settle for a higher window, so I changed the child's interior voice to *"I looked out the window and faces were passing by."* The luminous and frightening spider became our *emotional equivalent* for the child's feelings of powerlessness and betrayal. As the molester removes her clothes (not shown because from where she stands on the broken chair, her point-of-view reveals the man's torso from neck to hip) the shot cuts to the spider in closeup and the child's voice—*my* voice remembering—*"Cobwebs have no spiders he said. I'll cut off your head if you tell anybody."*

I had thought about this scene for several years—how it would look, what elements would be incorporated—but when the time came to direct it, I truly had to face my four-year-old self. I took with me into the basement all the fortifications I could gather. When my friend signed the property release for the use of her basement, she told me how she was molested by a priest when she was six years old, growing up in Chile. I took *her* story into the basement. I brought in (out of camera range) the mother of the child I was filming because my mother was not in the original basement of 1939. The molester is played by my adult son and the fact that this man whom I love, whom I gave birth to was the stand-in for a scary person from my childhood gave me command and power over a traumatic episode in my life. I was able to say to him, *"Move here," "Lift the chair from the wall," "Walk through again."* I could control this dear actor. And, because film is magic, my son is also one of the men who walks by the window. He is the inside man *and* the outside man looking in.

The film story, then, surpasses real life by transforming experience, clarifying intent, linking cause to effect, adding perspective, telescoping and/or combining memories, sorting the remembered from the forgotten *and* imposing narrative onto the experience.

In some respects a story—whatever the medium—cannot encompass all the truths of a life. In other respects the life, from which the story is being spun, is enlarged. This happens in the transformation of life to story. The characters become larger than the individuals, the story becomes clearer because the irrelevant, the trivial is abandoned. And always in the re-telling the present is imposed upon the past.

Each tale—*life* story, *literary* story and *film* story—is a mutation of the others, yet each exists independently of the others and of its creator. Are the stories true? After all, everything really happened, though not in the manner portrayed. *"Realism, in any case,"* says Godard, *"is never exactly the truth...behind the theater is life and behind life, the theater. My pointof departure was the imaginary and I discovered the real; but, behind the real there was the imaginary."* Each version of "Three Versions Of The Man In The Basement" is truthfully told. They are *my* truths—one is a true story from my childhood, the others are adult versions of the truth, arrived at through the imagination—something I could never have achieved were I not an artist with the desire to restructure my past.

Rachel Loden

ARCHAEOLOGY (AS IF THE PRESENT MATTERED)

In the dawn, armed with a burning patience,
we shall enter the splendid Cities.
— Rimbaud

Entering the lost city
had been the work of decades.
Only fragmentary maps survived the burning
of the ancient libraries,
and bits of text
enigmatic as runes.

These were presented
at the court of daylight
and to your dreams,
where broken clues
grew into bestiaries
of extravagant creatures,
and syllabic shards awoke
as riddles on your lips.

You worked slowly,
taking pains. You
pieced and pasted,
tore apart and rearranged,
invented geographies, and, failing,
wept yourself hoarse.
You were patient. How
could you be otherwise?
You had no choice.

Finally you took your scraps
and compass to the desert,
till something solid
touched your spade. Now,
as you work down to another level,
a burning patience brings to light
the old walled city that you made.

IN PRAISE OF DARKNESS

Before sleep, what is restless in you
rummages through its pockets,
as though on a nightstand
you could empty your whole life.

Your pockets sing like fishwives,
their hustled wares
a rack of monsters,
a basket of bright-colored bits

of scales and fur and wings.
At first light, surrender: you fall asleep
inside those soft and ample pockets,
knocked unconscious with cracked lullabies.

But on a night like any other night
you drift into a half-remembered place.
There is a quietness, as after
some mad chatter dies.

And you know it was a kind of vanity
that made you turn from happiness,
its mysteries unreckoned
in the dark, for you to praise.

THE CASTLE

If I come to you as some bitter herb,
if I come to you cold and wrinkled as the moon,
if I call to you, not even knowing I call,
like a she-cat lost and yowling in the rain,

if I immolate before you,
if my head is filled with water,
if you are stone when you look on me,
and yet you stay to be my mirror,

then my lap is filled with golden apples,
and I am seven daughters dancing
in the all-night place beneath the fathers,
I am seven pairs of threadbare slippers in the morning.

Renée Freiheit

NOW THAT THE HOUSE IS QUIET

The most wrenching, difficult act I have committed happened sometime before I was two years old. It was also the most self-destructive, but I believe that I chose it because my options were limited. The brain is perched like a spider in the web of all my nerves. Its job is to receive information from the outside world, and process it, and spur the body to act for survival. What if survival means the opposite of taking it all in?

At two, my father was too much for me to understand or predict. With the smell of his alcohol breath close to my face, he might kiss me and laugh if my mother was around. He might stumble in late at night and stick his fingers inside me. He might be sober and buy me an ice cream, while still looking at me as if I were naked. I thought he might devour me, but that I would get into trouble if I screamed when he came near me; it wasn't polite. I learned to take my senses and turn them off, put them to sleep, turn them inward. It was either that or continue to feel fear every time I saw him, and shake whenever I heard footsteps, thinking it might be him.

In exchange for a comforting numbness, I became a little spacey, a bit jumpy. Because I didn't allow myself to utter a peep against my father, to even see him, I failed to be specific about my fear or to name it. I thought that anyone might hurt me at any time, and I didn't believe that anyone could be predictable, could be counted on not to explode in anger. Since my father didn't match the dads I saw on T.V., and since I was told, "You may not be able to tell, but he loves you a lot," I believed that something was wrong with my eyes or my brain to make me perceive violence where others didn't see it.

Today, as I write this, I am sitting in the alcove of a coffee shop. A man walks around the corner toward me. I assume that his glance at me means he is biding his time, closing in on me with agonizing slowness. When he takes down his pants, knocks me out of my chair and goes through the act, I will not be able to scream. I have to convince myself that this scene probably won't happen. If a woman bumps into me while I wait for the subway, I assume she will push me onto the tracks without a second thought. So I stay away from the tracks. When a man looks at me, says something about my appearance, I smile apologetically, hoping he will forgive me for not wanting to suck him off right now. I smile constantly and laugh frequently, and I'm known for this among my friends, who say I have a sunny outlook. I think, however, that the smile is an attempt to appease the potential abusers that I believe surround me, saying, "Look, I am such easy game. I won't even resist. If it's the struggle and thrashing that gets you hard, the cries of pain, I will only lie as still as a corpse. So pass me by." This is deeply embedded in me. To make myself conscious of it and write about it is challenging and also pretty embarrassing.

I have been writing stories since the second grade, filling in the gaps with a fantasy world. This was a world all my own, populated with close little girl friends who didn't have parents, who fought robots and invaders and saved civilizations. There were no men with booming voices in my stories, and there was no physical contact. Now when I look back on these stories and read between the lines, it is the only record I have of how I felt then. Writing helped me to work at creating worlds that made sense, and characters with predictable traits who grew and become more honest and more brave, where the good girls won in the end. When my mother bought me a typewriter in fifth grade, the one I still have, she threw me a lifeline.

She and I couldn't connect to talk about how we were feeling. She was also seeking safety. She would raise her voice to say, "Smile! Why don't you smile?" I began to feel that my self-imposed numbness was a sin. Eager to please, I learned ways to break through my own shell without dealing with what had made it necessary. I am ashamed to admit that I threatened myself like I had been threatened ("If you tell, I'll..."). I wasn't naturally able to focus on much besides story-telling and poetry in school, but to become perfect, less deserving of punishment, I tried to excel in everything. I learned math by repeatedly biting the tips of my fingers, holding my breath, punching my head, arms and legs, all in order to draw out the sharpness of concentration. By eighth grade I had to be more subtle. My friends were beginning to notice my behavior and tension and asked me why I was so angry with myself. I pulled my hair more discreetly in algebra class. I clenched my stomach muscles to feel nausea. I said, "You suck, you are shit," silently, all to rouse myself so that I would absorb. When I took piano lessons, there was a toy gun that I held to my head when I couldn't follow the notes. No wonder I quit — the playing held little pleasure, and the songs all seem sarcastic.

Today I am twenty-three. I moved eight hundred miles from my home town to escape my father. I tried and failed at family therapy. I have had brief, lucid conversations with my mother about my father's problems, which she forgets about immediately after we speak. I know about that, so I take notes. I take prescription pills for depression with some regret that I can't do it all "on my own," but I know that the self-destructive urge to step in traffic and shock myself awake is still within me, and the greatest revenge is to stay alive.

Yesterday I spoke with my mother on the phone. As usual, trying to deny her own confusion, she wanted peace in the family and asked me to just say hello to my father. He grabs the receiver and says hello in his cartoon voice, and hello is virtually all he says. He asks how I am doing and doesn't wait for an answer. We are like two different species, unable to communicate. I am sure we have a lot in common, but I don't want to know about it.

After hearing his voice, I feel alone and betrayed, and sad that my mother falls back on convention, using me to prop up her illusions of a happy family. His voice, even now, undresses me and ignores me as human all at once. Over the next weeks, I know it will all be replayed in my head. I will have nightmares about everyone I ever loved speaking another language, failing to see me, trying to destroy me with misunderstandings. I will hyperventilate on the street when a middle-aged man with dark hair bumps up against me. I will watch a bus coming toward me as I wait on the curb, and part of me will push, say "You're going to die..." just so I can feel the dim resistance of another part that says, "No," the muted but still present life force. I will abuse and threaten myself in ways that friends don't ever notice, so that I know that I'm alive. And I'll smile more than usual to increase my feeling of isolation. But the part of me that is able to cry or has been lovingly kind to children will check a book on incest out from the library, and I will start to come up for air. I'll be exhausted like the last time, but at least it's getting more familiar, although I don't know how it will end.

Richard Ernie Reed

THE DAY DAD SHRANK

It was in the somber side of fifty years,
on a cloudy Wednesday morning,
when the realization hit me,
lightly, a bitter, wormy acorn
fallen from an old oak tree,
reminding me of what I was leaning on.

His shape always covered the sun,
a cool shadow clouding my world,
stretching to the farthest edges of
vision, hiding the storm's rumbling
flashes of fire.

I never knew when a brittle branch would fall,
or lightning strike from the thunderheads of his smile.
Few childhood memories remain, only nervous tics
and vague feelings of dread. I assumed it was
happy, uneventful, except for hard hands
beating regularly like a clock, creating echoes
of distant drumming that still vibrate in
the deep seismic zone of dreams.

He was small but strong, the oldest of eight,
the little man of a drunken sharecropper's household,
dodging hugs and hits, streetwise to
anger, fear and retribution. Childhood snaps
show me even smaller, my smile
a sliver of unease between dry lips,
as he watched somewhere
behind the Kodak, clicking away.

He didn't have time for fun, except
once he did go swimming, doing
cartwheels in the water until he almost drowned.
They carried him home. It seems drowning was
easy for him, swimming was hard, and he knew it.
I often wonder what another father would have
been like, but then I would have been another son.

It took the long-dead acorn, eaten inside
by worms, to fall and break open my mind's eye.
It hurts, images flash, my amazement is genuine.
I see him now, through a glass broken by reality.
He has somehow shrunk, become even more of a
child than I ever was. The tough old tree that loomed
so huge is now a bonsai, dwarfed, planted in a
shallow pot, gnarled roots digging into the dirt
with white knuckles, just barely holding on.

As he grows smaller, I grow taller,
an optical illusion as artificial as my memories.
We glance at one another, astonished,
not talking much. He sees the change,
his eyes mostly blind, that confused,
boyish smile on his lips. Walking on
arthritic legs, holding onto my reluctant
arm, he shuffles down the long hallway.
Even through the cataracts, he can see
the light at the end. His feet drag, forcing
him to take one last angry, incredulous
look at me through tears that seem
to break out for no reason.

I help him along, pumped up with something
like courage, the cautious ecstasy of freedom.

Then I slow our pace,
thinking
thirty years ahead,
wondering if I will be then
as small
as
he is
now,
confused equally by
the fiction of memory and fact,
never able to fully
explain,
as someone else helps,
growing big as

I shrink,
urging
me
toward the
glowing
door.

LOOK AT ME.

Walked by the mirror, caught
you out the corner of my eye.
Thought I didn't see you,
but I did, kid.

You're so smart, sliding
by like that, furtively,
slinking lightly,
making no sound.

But the wind moves, heart
skips just a little,
you aren't so far gone
I can't see.

Look at me, stop in your
flight, just once, so
I might know who, you
and me, who we really are.

Little scared kid, bent low,
evading something heavy and
hard, a bland, blind smile
pinched between thin lips.

You still there under those
long lashes? I catch flashes
of blue, brilliant winter
crystals covering angelwings.

Lately, I spend hours watching,
waiting for you to show, thinking
maybe to catch you peeking at
an angle through the silver.

I plot to slow you down,
open you to our need,
make your sky shine, twin
beams burn darkness between us.

If only I could move
in front of your guarded gaze,
so we can square what is
within the circle of what can be.

Look at me, please, look at me,
I want to know, after all these
years of timid intimacy, whether
somehow we both can share the pain.

Molly Fisk

THE VIEW FROM THE OTHER SIDE OF HEALING
AN INTERVIEW WITH LOUISE WISECHILD

One Sunday afternoon, at a small coffee shop in the Northern California town of Santa Rosa, I interviewed Louise Wisechild, well-known writer and healer. I was hoping to discover that recovery from sexual abuse is possible, and to find out what happens in the final stages of healing. I read my first question:

"What is your life like now? Are you able to trust people, enjoy your sexuality, have a spiritual connection, be a good parent, and so on?"

"Yes!" —Much laughter—"Next question?"

"What was the hardest part of your recovery?"

"Oh, I'd say the first eighteen years."

(Wait a mintue—did I hear that right? She said *yes?* She enjoys her *sexuality*?)

Louise explained: "I had a really incredible change in feeling sexual, especially after the memory process, when I never thought I was going to be sexual again. It went through stages. No sex at all, never-care-if-I-have-it-again when I broke up with my lover. Then I was celibate for a while, and then it felt like my sexuality kind of burst out. I got involved with someone and had a very hot time sexually, but not a heart connection. Then, when I met my current partner, my heart and sexuality were really joined together, which is a wonderful thing."

I interviewed Louise Wisechild when she was on a book signing and workshop tour. She had driven five hours from the Central California Valley, where she had given a reading from her new book, *The Mother I Carry*, the night before. I was curious to see if advanced healing shows on a person's face, but she looked like any other friendly woman who had just spent too much time in a car.

Louise is a writer, musician, body-worker, teacher, and lecturer, specializing in working with adult survivors of childhood abuse. Her first book, *The Obsidian Mirror: An Adult Healing From Incest*, published in 1988 (Seal Press), describes her memories and her healing process. One of the first personal descriptions of recovering memories to appear, it is now regarded as a healing classic. With an inner cast of characters representing the different aspects of her personality, Louise leads the reader through her own journey to recovery.

"The process of having memories was so extraordinary—the physicality of it and the way that you can be there again in every way . . . I started writing *The Obsidian Mirror* . . . because the process of having memories was so incredible and severe," Louise explained.

Louise had her first memory in a therapy session in 1977; she was describing her urge to hide in the closet when she suddenly had an image of her grandfather's penis and felt overwhelming nausea. Her therapist didn't follow up on this image, and Louise didn't mention it again.

The second time was in 1983, during hypnotherapy to stop smoking. This time Louise investigated the memory. She went back into therapy and had new memories come up weekly for about a year. She counts the steadiness and good boundaries of this therapist, whom she continued to see for eight years, as one of the most positive effects on her recovery.

Another great support was her writing. "Writing had always been a survival thing for me. Because I felt so alienated and isolated I was most comfortable being alone and writing." In addition to writing *The Obsidian Mirror*, Louise is the editor of an anthology, *Who Was Lost Is Remembered: Healing from Incest Through Creativity*, and author, most recently, of *The Mother I Carry: A Memoir of Healing From Emotional Abuse.*

I asked Louise how she perceived advanced healing, and she said taking care of herself—which we defined as eating healthy food, staying clean, getting the laundry done, going to the doctor regularly, not acting out or abusing substances of choice—was better and easier. "That was a big sign. For a long time to take care of myself even reasonably was really hard. I'd go along taking semi-good care of myself, and then I would take really rotten care of myself for a while. I couldn't sustain it. I find that my preference now is to eat a certain way.

"It's all right for me to feel good and I think that it took me a long time to learn that. That's been really great.

"I'm a lot more aware of what I say to myself. The critic, from the abuse, was so strong and everything was life-threatening. What did other people think, and how did I look, and what were they saying? [I was] living outside . . . my own body and trying to see what other people saw. Now I hear that voice—I call her Sarah—and she's changed what she's saying, but also, I can tell if I'm starting to get tense or if I'm not liking myself very much. I've developed a relationship with her. Because I use that inner voice model, it's gotten a lot more natural to consult myself.

"There's also a sense of being fed more continuously. No matter what's going on, I'm aware that the kids in me can find something that's delightful or interesting or in-the-moment. I can stop and have a minute-long experience if that's all the time I have. I used to think I had to have a whole day to do anything."

These changes didn't take place all at once for Louise, but she had moments of feeling better than she'd ever felt. "A spaciousness. Room to take risks. I really like to sing and perform, and I feel like I really had the space to try things. Not like before when I was afraid to leave my apartment."

She also talked about the strength of her spiritual connection: "One thing about the spiritual part of my life is that it is continually growing, in contrast to the rigid system my parents had, which was essentially passive. What distinguishes my sense of spirituality is that it supports growth and awareness. My experience has been that there is a creative, loving, passionate force—I call it the goddess sometimes and also the creative spirit—which is a part of me and a part of everything else. I access it through meditation and what I call contemplation—thinking about what's going on. Not 'Why did this happen to me?' but 'What can I make of this? What is there to learn here?'

"It is only in *expressing* my spirituality that I can sense it. Singing, for example, is very spiritual to me. And when I'm expressing this spirituality, it pleases the children in me. Then, too, because it's an active process, there's a trust that when things happen that are difficult, there's a way to get through them."

Louise is currently in an "eclectic collection of therapies, mostly leaderless." This includes a dream group, which she's been in for six years, and a voice/improvisation/movement group; both of these encompass personal growth work. She sees a therapist for "occasional tune-ups—mostly to talk about issues that come up from being so public in my work, which is also a kind of tonic."

I asked Louise what she would say to survivors who are still slogging through the toughest parts of the recovery process.

She replied, "Believe yourself. [Don't] let anyone else tell you who you are or what happened to you. In some ways, there's a lot more help and support now than when I was starting the process and, in some ways, there are more dangers. It's important not to get stuck in a diagnosis. People are writing all sorts of books on how it *should* be. One of the gifts of going through it when I did was that I was able to follow my own process. So be true to yourself."

▣ Jackie Warren-Moore

I AM WOMAN WHO SHOUTS

I am woman who shouts
I wonder why the sky shakes with my voice
I hear the thunder within me
I see the clouds rush to hiding
I want to shout of injustice — banish it from
the earth.
I am woman who shouts

I pretend there is magic in my speaking —
power to change
I feel the sting of rain upon my face.
I touch my fingers to wounds so deep
there is no bottom.
I worry the pain will swallow me
like open earth.
I cry out, my shout cracking the sky
like lightning.
I am woman who shouts.

I understand the earth's movement.
I say the words that will free me.
I dream peace — quiet —
I bank the fire that burns deep
in my soul.
I hope for the power to dream again
I am woman who shouts.

FOR SHADA

It takes only one woman to break the cycle,
Circle of pain that haunted you through foster nights
a hunger so deep
only your heartbeat and your own strength nourished you.
Only your loud laughter and your razor sharp mind guided
you through

traps that lay in wait for you.
Through the anger and the tears
laughter and pain
you molded your dreams, forged them
by hand
and rinsed them in your tears.
Walk proud,
Woman Who Leads,
she who broke the back of the cycle.
Shout to the world
your new name. . .
Woman Who Dreams.

DAUGHTERS

Red tipped triangle of the Ancestors
Misty guides support and urge me forward on dusty
    African trails.
I move toward the twin peaks — green breast thrust to the sky.
Travelling down, down, deeper down to the waiting
    valley between.
The brook runs like glistening sweat between the globes.

I find myself there. Waiting and laughing. Holding hands
    with my
daughter. Loving her as I never loved myself.
Little girl laughter in three's.
Old self.
New self.
Daughter.

We are three.
We are one.
Splashing water that falls in triangles against
    soft brown skin.
Shadows form as I prepare to leave.
I am reluctant to leave them there.
We join hands — old self, new self, daughter.
Red tipped triangle of the Ancestors skipping home.

Homer Mitchell

A TREATMENT, A TREAT

We are working, healing
with bittersweet, with fantasy
those hot seasaw years

Remember—you home alone
a seismic disturbance
that reluctance to run?

The doctor is in
What a surprising touch
Just what you need—

A pretend future
Quiet. Press here
Don't stop.

▣ Sue Doro

FATHER POEMS: COMING TO GRIPS WITH THE PAST

...My father was a union member and he talked about voting for Democrats. He also was a racist, a wife beater and a child abuser. At the age of 62, shortly after retiring, he died of heart failure from washing down too many real pain pills with half pints of Coronet brandy. I've written two poems that included him. The first was called, simply, "The Father Poem." It concerned living and dying in the working class in this country. People who had problems dealing with memories of their fathers, related to it. They'd come to me after readings with tears in their eyes, thanking me for giving them some words to connect with their own unspoken thoughts.

Then about four years ago, I stopped reciting it in public. The events were historically intact, but there were whole sections of the poem I couldn't live with. I knew that I was lying to myself. To understand the importance of this choice, I have to say that the poem was considered to be my "best" work by many people.

There continued to be requests to publish it. I felt torn, and confused. On the one hand the poem was technically good, and, in fact, some people seemed to be "helped" by it. I should have been proud and anxious for an editor to want to publish any of my poems. I ended up telling myself that it was a poem about someone else's father, and let it go at that. *I* just wouldn't read it anymore. But the poem followed me. It wouldn't let me alone. I decided that I had to face it. I had to take control of the poem.

In the original version, I spoke about what I think I *should* have done as my father's daughter. Things like sticking by him and fighting side by side against "the rich men who caused my father to..."

"The Father Poem" was written in 1972. My political awareness based on working-class, Franklin D. Roosevelt Democrat background, tilted noticeably leftward during the late 60's. I had been forced into the role of a single parent after a thirteen year "perfect" high school marriage ended abruptly in abandonment. I was trying to figure out how to survive and raise five kids without the financial (or any other) support of an X-husband. The Vietnam war, women's movement and poor people's struggles, had touched Milwaukee's south side and the idea of female oppression, war and economic suffering seemed to fit me perfectly. I was angry at my "X" and at the "system," but not at a dead father.

It seemed that I just couldn't let the rich and powerful win yet another victory. Screwed up as my father was, I felt if I allowed even a bit of blame to rest at his feet, millionaires all over the world would smile gleefully, relishing the idea that they were being released of any blame. I had it figured out. It seemed plain to me that the pain he dished out to his family was not his fault.

Twenty years later, in the '90's, time and life experience have given me a less simplistic political analysis of social problems. I still maintain, however "old fashioned" it may sound, that the capitalist patriarchal social and economic system has a strangle hold on the everyday people. I believe it needs to be changed. I believe we're affected as a group and individually... in our working and want-to-be-working lives, in our relationships with each other at work and in our homes. The political *is* personal.

In the initial revision period of "The Father Poem," I found myself examining something I had ignored, denied and wouldn't even have allowed myself to consider when I first wrote the poem. It was the fact that my father had choices. Why didn't I think about this earlier? My father hadn't changed since the poem was written. He was still dead. Our family history was the same. Apparently I was the one who had changed.

In the years between 1972 and 1992, I had been employed in factories just like the one my father worked in. As a blue collar woman, (the only female machinist in the three shops where I worked during that time), I was able to develop friendships with my co-workers. Many of the men were victims of industrial injuries and illnesses. Most of them were Democrats. Most of them belonged to a union. We had a common struggle. It was "us against the bosses." We had a yearning for more control over our labor. We wished for more time off to do whatever we wanted. We could band together to make decisions that affected our work lives, whether it was fighting against a vicious foreman or putting our heads together to figure out a machining problem. Our tool boxes were not necessarily individual property, although they were respected. The real physical danger of our jobs forged team-work bonds for survival.

Even though these working-class men contended with some of the same unsafe working conditions and health problems as my father, they were not cruel to each other or to their families. I was introduced to the people close to them. Friendships developed that I still hold close to my heart. I spent time in their homes. They visited my home. They met my family. I saw the love these men demonstrated for their families. There was love in my own family.

By this time, the children and I were living with the man who would become my second husband. He worked 7:00 A.M. to 3:30 P.M. as a machinist at another factory. I grappled with the night shift at Allis Chalmers Tractor shop. We had differences, but we struggled through them together. We were partners in every sense of the word. There was a persistence that we had in common. A way of sticking out hard situations to the end... of resolving what you can and letting go when you can't see what else to do. And probably, most importantly, we tried not to take our work problems out on each other. It was difficult, especially being on opposite shifts. He would be sleeping at 1:00 A.M. when I'd get home from work. I'd call each week night on my 8 o'clock break, and we taped messages to each other on an old tape recorder we kept on the kitchen table. He took care of the house and kids when I worked "nights." It stretched our relationship almost to breaking. Some of the kids tried to see how much they could get away with, since either one or the other of their "set" of parents was missing most of the time. We got along, but it wasn't a T.V. family situation comedy with a neatly wrapped up conclusion at the end of each half hour. It was damn hard. Some of the endings were happy. Some weren't.

In the factories where I worked for almost thirteen years, I also saw one or two men who were dangerous, self-destructive and unpredictable. They were not the norm. They'd perform their jobs in a suicidal manner, burning up machine motors and breaking gear teeth in their frantic rush to work faster. Their accident rate was ten times the average, especially the afternoons when they's come back to work after lunch break smelling like the taverns at the top of the hill. If they stayed at work to eat, they'd curse wives and girl friends for packing some kind of food they didn't apparently like that day. They laughed about how they'd "knock 'em around to teach 'em a lesson." They were generally individualistic and politically backward in their gut responses to oppressive work situations.

When a lay-off was in the wind, and management ordered speed ups in production, they would work even faster. They became hostile, suspicious, and even more dangerous to be near. In the factory's communal atmosphere where co-workers helped each other on a regular basis, they forced us to stay away from them through their anti-social actions. The closer it came to the lay off date, the more irrational their choice of solutions became. If working faster wouldn't stop the lay-off clock from ticking, it must be something else. It must be *somebody* else. They blamed everyone who wasn't a white male, and said they shouldn't be working there. We were taking their jobs away.

I learned to avoid these people like everyone did. They could not be "reasoned" with. I saw that they chose to act the way they did. They were not robots whose arms, mouths and legs were attached to strings. We all worked in the same factory. We were not all reacting to the worsening work situation in the manner that they were. Even some of the guys who went up the hill to drink at lunch time didn't act like they did. Though they were frightened, sad individuals, we held them accountable for their actions. They had no right to pass on their own personal feelings of oppression by persecuting others.

Neither did my father.

I began to understand that my own personal political beliefs did not contradict my right to hold him accountable. My father chose to isolate himself from the rest of his family. He wouldn't listen to people who tried to help him. I remember one doctor that made a house visit when he was off sick, telling him he wouldn't give him any more prescriptions because he wasn't following the dosage. My father chased him out of our house yelling obscenities. My mother told him more than once to quit his job and go on disability. He said she was crazy. I remember one of the very few times I was alone with him and not afraid. We were walking to the hardware store together. I must have been 4 or 5 years old, because I wore a red cape that I loved, and a navy blue felt hat with a brown and red feather, and the outfit didn't fit me by the time I started school. I remember looking up at him while we walked, and asking him why he acted so mean all the time. He kept on walking, and answered, "because I want to."

Understanding my father has meant examining his personal choices and his decaying health made worse by the horrible and dangerous conditions he worked under. His own childhood suffering must have also played a part. I remember him telling stories of how his father beat him with a horse buggy whip on a regular basis.

I have yet to face the issue of my mother's responsibility in the arguments and chaos in our household. As an adult, I can't separate her misery and sadness from her own personal choices. Her torment was too much a part of mine. She was also physically abused by my father. But why did she appear to relish prolonging the arguments? Why didn't she take the kids and go back to her home town to live with relatives or friends until she could get on her feet financially?

I can't answer my own questions. It's too easy to judge her by current social standards. It was a different era. She was a battered woman in a time before the term was invented. Did the situation she found herself in allow her to consider other options? Would she have listened if she did have help? Apparently, she just couldn't do it, for whatever reasons.

At the same time as my own blue collar experience was helping me rethink my father's choices, something else was happening in my life. I was beginning to remember details from my childhood that I had formerly pushed deep inside. I was fourteen when I watched helplessly as my mother died on the dining room floor. Graphic scenes from her death haunted me on a daily basis. Sometimes these thoughts would grab hold of me in waves of real physical as well as mental pain. Memories of my father coming towards me screaming that he'd kill me if I tried to get help for my mother would cause my neck and shoulders to freeze into tightly wound muscle spasms. My stomach would ache. My nerves were constantly on edge. Sometimes I had real problems just being where I was at a given moment. I drifted off, felt disorganized, got lost in the past. It was disconcerting and sometimes actually dangerous, especially if I was driving a car or running the machines at work.

Finally, there came a time when I ceased to deny the effects of my past. My second husband and I had been together for seventeen years by this time. We had moved to California. Our kids were grown and on their own. Every time we agreed on an issue, be it about relating to the kids, issues "back home," handling money or work questions, it seemed I would end up doing the opposite of what we had originally decided together without telling him that I had actually changed my mind. I did not understand myself. Why did I stubbornly latch on to an opinion when I knew that I was wrong. Why couldn't I utter a simple "thank you" without thinking that a piece of myself was being torn away. Why couldn't I accept praise without wanting to hide? Why was I—a writer—unable to describe how she *felt*. My actions and his reactions were pulling us apart. I loved him and he loved me, but we argued constantly. Our relationship was at stake.

I began to work on myself as if I were machining a piece of steel that had been scratched and marred by outside forces. In the beginning I went to the library and got books about children of alcoholics. A half year later I tried therapy for the first time, but the therapist and I didn't "click." My husband continued to encourage me. He was also working on things in himself that he wanted to change. We decided to stick it out together.

Then I found Sandra. I was referred to her by a friend who also was seeing her for profession help. Sandra became my engine lathe of understanding. I was, at the same time, the machinist and the cutting tool. Hot metal chips flew into the air as the damaged metal was removed. Some of the pieces landed back on my bare skin, burning into my flesh, but I didn't stop. Some of the hot chips of my past ricocheted off me and landed on my husband. The work is still not finished.

And so it was that when I revisited "The Father Poem" my eyes, heart and new political awareness all allowed me to view my father and his actions in a more realistic light. I accepted the fact that he had choices. And even though his choices were colored by the effects that capitalism had on him, personally, as a working-class blue collar man, I realized that he still had to be held accountable. I realized that to say to the world that my father "couldn't help it" would be unfair to the other working-class men I knew and admired, not to mention, personally dishonest.

A short time ago, I read the new version of "The Father Poem" aloud for the first time. Again, people came to me expressing their gratitude for giving their feelings a voice. This time, however, many more *women* verbalized their *relief*. They said that the poem gave them permission to feel that they didn't have to forgive in order to understand.

THE FATHER POEM (TWO)

my father,
dark gray,
dusty factory father,
left with one lung
from filthy air,
aching with rheumatism,
from winter cold air
blowing on sweaty shoulders.

my father,
cursing your job, through us,
your family,
mean to my mother
my brother, my sister,
me.

yelling, coughing.
spitting angry yellow,
green and red.

my father, swallowing pills
to keep on your feet.
swallowing pills
to get to sleep.

my father,
two months into retirement,
an uncashed check
on the kitchen table,
found dead,
by the lady who ran
the downstairs tavern.

my father, dead,
your body melting
into the floor boards
near a shoe box
of assorted pills,
an empty brandy bottle,

and a bucket of spit
lined with newspaper.
your pain is finished now.

-2-

my father, dead but not gone,
alive but not living,
I remember you,
coming home
from a ten hour work day,
taking off your glasses
to reveal white circles
of sunken eyes
surrounded by soot,
because sometimes
you were too tired
to clean up at work,
in the washroom
your union fought for.

on those nights,
I remember
when the white circles
were around your eyes,
and your clothes
smelled like Johnnie's Bar,
you'd spit on the floor
and at mamma,
swearing, as you flung what was left
of your pay check,
and she would pick up the scattered bills,
the rolling coins,
and tuck them in her apron pocket,
while you kept on
cursing her for being there,
and I hid
behind the doorway,
not wanting to leave her
alone with you,
but too afraid
to stand next to her
and fight.

my father dead but not gone,
alive but not living,
were you always mean?
or were there days
I never knew?
lost years on a farm,
when you were a little boy,
summers gone loving
in the sun with the woman
who would become my mother.

-3-

days of slow drives to Milwaukee
in a truck full of fresh farm eggs
and sand stuffed chickens,
to make them weigh more when you got there.
old days when you were the man
my mother loved,
before you worked
in a rich man's factory,
and taverns became your second home.

potatoes-in-the-cellar days,
when both of you were young and new
and lived in Berlin, Wisconsin,
and went to band concerts in the park,
gathered hickory nuts,
and knew everyone in town.

what did you feel
when the depression
robbed you of your business?

how scared were you
to come to a big city
with a wife and 2 babies?
how guilty did you feel
for leaving your oldest child behind?

and how crazy did it make you
to be a family provider
who could not provide

in a system that demands it
as part of manhood?

my father,
a good welder,
proud to be
one of the best
in your department.
sealing seams
of World War II bombs,
from inside their smoky guts.
welding slabs of blue metal,
to create corn silos,
for farms you would only dream of,
frames for trucks
you could never afford.

-4-

how did it feel
when a time came,
and your shaky hands
and watering eyes
couldn't keep the torch steady?

on the day you collapsed at work,
the shop doctor gave you
a prescription for pain pills,
and a week of sick leave.
when you returned,
you found you'd been transferred
to the tool crib.

your use as a profit machine,
was over.
a welding career finished,
your new assignment:
to hand others their tools.

you were sick, and old at fifty-five,
and I feared and hated
and did not understand you.
did you feel bad

after swearing at me
for not emptying your bucket
fast enough?
did you feel ashamed
when you cursed and blamed me
for mamma's dying,
and your only son's death?
and for not being able
to breathe hear see
or walk without a cane?

after mamma died, you wanted me
to take her place.
I stayed late at school each night,
until the janitor made me leave.

you'd come home to sit in your red rocker
by the window,
looking out on Lisbon Avenue,
and you'd rock and talk
to yourself
about corn silos,
and dead relatives.

-5-

did you ever think
of the man you used to be?
did you ever question
the choices that you made?

were you sorry
for the pain
you put your family through,
the misery no child should endure?

did you wonder, as i do,
how much was from the rich man?
how much,
from you?

my father,
dark gray dusty factory father,

dead but not gone,
alive but not living,

for thirty years
you had a clock number.
a.o. smith company
knew you by it.

as for me,

I knew you
by your anger,
your choices,

and our communal pain.

⊠ ⊠ ⊠

"Focus" is the first new poem I've written about my father since 1972. The dream I describe happened. Its sequences combined the reality of memory with dream fantasies. My father *did* have his picture taken for an advertisement. The repaired snapshot *is* included in the old family album I took when I ran away from home as a teenager. My father *did* mentally, physically and sexually abuse me as a child. I really did awake from the dream, laughing, and feeling flushed, vibrant and determined to record it. The words flowed fast and easily. Writing it was my personal victory.

The original title of the poem was "Entries and Exits," but it didn't seem to fit after I began to write this accompanying essay. When I thought about how my working class background had effected "Focus," I decided that the topic of my family and its history could not have a "exit." The family events I'm aware of, and those that continue to open to me, will be with me as long as I have memories.

My family was like a team of injured players, needing each other to finish a game we never wanted to be in. Some team members died trying....

FOCUS

write about it she
said the dream gray
red the man
his penis entering

his features
resembling
a movie star
suggesting
my father's face
was handsome

he was a sears roebuck
model some time
around 1920
before he traveled
to milwaukee to become a
factory worker

in between the small town
chicken and egg enterprise
when my mother was
not yet
his wife

she kept a
picture cut out of a
catalog page featuring
him dressed in a
knee length dark
overcoat buckled at
the waist

collar wide lapeled a
sears smile on his face
he was bare-headed one
hand at his side the
other tucked against
his chest like
napoleon the image

torn in
several pieces
one of the times
my mother
verified her anger

reattached like a puzzle
pasted on a piece of
yellowed cardboard
preserved in our
family album
before my child
eyes could see it all
happen

the handsome man
is talking now
requesting
the return of his penis

seems it got stuck
when I broke it off
at the root like
the fat gray stem
of one of those
strange sea plants
sticking up from
the ocean floor
blood red tipped

I couldn't feel
anything all
I knew was I
didn't want it in me
so I simply pinched it
off with my thumb and
index finger there
wasn't any physical pain
involved although the man
appeared concerned about
his penis

while
I was in turn
interested
in the fact that
it remained inside
now that I had
severed the organ from
its source

so with a casualness of
someone not myself I
plucked it out with
the same thumb and finger
and it felt
pleasant removing it
in fact I did enjoy
an orgasm at this point
returning the artifact

watching with
head tilted curiosity
while he attempted to
reconnect the thing
to the stump above
his testicles the entire
area favoring segmented
clay characters
in animated cartoons

it was indeed funny it
made me
laugh

Billie Custock

TOMORROW'S YOUR BIRTHDAY

What present will do?
How many you want?
Three, one or two?
So many to choose from
Which one will it be?
Shall it be all the shame
You've given to me?
Or the guilt and the fears?
Or the sadness and tears?
Sleepless nights?
Or embarrassing days?
The brutal words?
Or the furious ways?
You gave so much
I'm not sure what's right
Which gifts you deserve
Wrapped up real tight

Your birthday is here
I'm glad you are not !!!

Although my father had been dead for over fourteen years, the pain and the terror were still fresh in my mind and heart. One of the healing rituals that I did after writing this poem, (using my non-dominant hand as the wounded inner child), was to use the Hallmark personalized card system printing this poem on a birthday card. On the back of the card I wrote:

This is personalized just for you by

Your wounded daughter, Billie

Patricia L. Nichol

THE TREE HOUSE

There are degrees of repression, ranging from memory unaccompanied by feeling to total loss of memory. Much of my childhood is a great, blank nothingness, punctuated by impressions of being stalked and watched; glimpses of the process of dissociation, and flash images of incest experiences. Set in the midst of this desolation is an event that occurred when I was ten, an event I always remembered, but never had any feelings about until four years ago, a couple of months before I began to remember that I was an incest survivor.

The summer I was ten, my family moved to Greeley, Colorado. We lived that summer in a rented house with berry bushes lining the back yard. My parents soon purchased a house, and we moved into it about the time that school began. It was a lovely, two-story house. One day, my father took my twin brothers (four years younger than I) and me into the back yard to a huge tree house. To my ten-year-old eyes, it was magical, unbearably beautiful.

He pointed to the tree house, then to the steps leading up to it—boards nailed to the side of the tree—and said, "I just wanted you to see me do this," and he tore off the boards. My father probably meant to show us how much he wanted to protect us. I, however, did not experience any love in his behavior. I was so devastated that I went away, removing my soul from my body and floating around for months thereafter. Much of my memory for years afterwards was lost.

I always remembered that incident as something that had merely happened, almost as if it had happened to someone else. For four years now, I've lived with reawakened feelings and the realization that I dissociated in order to live through the pain.

What really happened—as I experienced it—that day?

I saw a magical tree house. I wanted to climb to that tree house, away from the insufferable terror and barrenness of my life; I wanted out of childhood. I saw the only means of getting to my safe place getting torn away step by step. Each board represented something: hope, aspiration, adventure, escape. And as each board was torn away, something was torn away in my soul.

Under therapeutic hypnosis, I was taken back to that day at the tree house. Even then, forty years later, I could not bear the pain, and my therapist had to have me move from being a participant to becoming an observer.

A lot happened when I was ten: my family moved, my father committed incest against me once more, the tree house steps to my place of safety were torn down, and I created a fantasy world which I then began to inhabit much of the time in order to survive. I know now that the fantasy world was both a means of blocking my incest memories, and a preliminary step toward the formation of multiple personalities. I remember walking across my grandparents' kitchen thinking, "If I can live through ten, I can live through anything."

And I did.

Today I have a fig tree outside my bedroom window. It's hardly an oak tree, but I love every branch and leaf on it, for it is my tree. Every morning I wake up and see my tree. *My tree.*

I've created a safe place in my mind: a tree house. I sometimes retreat there when I want to feel safe. I write about the tree house and draw it regularly as a part of the process of healing.

My tree house.

My tree.

My life.

My soul.

My victory.

Jane Bailey

IT IS EASY TO BELIEVE IN THE LOVE OF TREES

Oaks, grandmothers of the park, hold the sky up
in gnarled hands. Willows mourn every motherless child.
This year our fig, mistaking a warm spring for summer
bears fruit twice. The first wrinkled orbs fall
like balloons once plump, now diminished by loss.
At summer solstice new womb-shaped fruits

small as baby toes appear, and I think when Eve
pulled those fig leaves away from the tree
she must have seen the unripe fruit and smiled
then taken the green hands of the Goddess in her own
and welcomed the stained-glass light of summer
unashamed as any mother prepared to give birth

to the world, one leaf not to hide but to shield
her seeds from sun, and two to shade her milk.
A friend says she has heard that after eaglets
learn to fly the mother places rocks in the nest
and I know that once a tree releases its offspring
they are not allowed to return. But this year

I am impressed by the motherly love of plants.
A kiwi with vines thick as arms embraces our house
and reaches out to neighbors. A peach sapling volunteer
implants itself in the garden. Yes, this year
I am in awe at how long trees can survive
without water, how fiercely and tenderly

they hold their leaves until it is time to let go,
how plants inhale relentless waste and offer
oxygen in return. Surely my own mother made a mistake,
was fooled by El Niño or an early summer, at least
I want to believe she was fooled, and not simply foolish

planting her daughters too close to her husband’s hot hands

where blossoms would fruit too early and fall.
But if nature can teach us anything
its secrets run in the veins of plants,
collect in the sap of trees. Observe
the second coming of figs, the way dried fruits
long removed from the tree plump up in water.

Anne Recker

MAYBE GOD IS AN OLD WOMAN

In the middle of memoir class, the teacher instructs us to free write. Pen to paper, she says, the first thing that pops into your mind. Keep writing. Don't allow the pen to leave the paper. I study the rain, trying to concentrate. In a week or two it will be Thanksgiving, I will write about being thankful. For what? I should be thankful that it's raining and not snowing, I decide. Although November rains in Iowa are bone chilling, it could be a blizzard I am watching. And then my pen stops. I don't feel grateful. When was the last time I felt grateful for anything? Anger leaves little space for much else.

It's been two years since my daughter, Christine, was diagnosed with Crohn's disease, a genetic disorder that causes severe inflammation in the GI tract. While not life threatening when treated, it is painful. There is no cure. She wears hospital gowns as often as party dresses, eats what she can tolerate, and gets on with her life while I seethe.

Pen to paper, a firm voice encourages. Think back. Write. Think back to what? To the jerks who masqueraded as doctors, who refused for years, to listen. The old men in white jackets who told me she was fine, who claimed I was an overprotective mother, who insinuated I'd somehow caused my daughter's illness. She's bulimic, they said. She's anorexic. Not until her colon perforated did they discover their error. Never once did they acknowledge it.

My fault. I can't deal with the guilt so I blame God. I know better, but I rage at Him regardless, raising my fist in fury and screaming at Him. God, how could You allow this to happen? She is only a child.

The teacher interrupts. What is your earliest memory? she asks. Go back, delve deep into your memories. I look at her uneasily as I remember why I'm taking this class in the first place. My grandfather has taken over my dreams. I did not know him well and yet he haunts my nights. It is always the same dream. He is sitting in a car, a vehicle that looks like an oversized Volkswagen. The car is parked on the church parking lot and Christine and I stop to admire its shiny chrome bumpers and black and green plaid seats. As we stand there, he reaches out to Christine. She steps closer and takes his hand.

I scream at her to get away from him. Don't you know he's dead, I warn.

She smiles at me, a smile too much like his. His hand is cold, Mom, she says. It cools my fever.

He wants you to die, I say.

He only wants our prayers, she says. He's come to ask for prayers.

Grandpa, I murmur, go away.

Not away, my teacher says.

I am embarrassed.

Go back, she says.

Grandpa was a short man with thin brown hair and big ears. He looked eternally sad and I thought, if it weren't for his startling blue eyes, he'd look just like a basset hound.

He was a farmer, not because he wanted to be but because it was all he knew. He went to school only long enough to learn to read, write and do figures. As a child, I didn't know him well, even though I'd spend a week or two each summer on his farm. I knew things about him though, things that made him seem more like a mystery than a grandfather. I'd heard whisperings of a nervous breakdown, of an alcohol problem.

Grandpa and Grandma married young and raised nine children. My mother was their oldest child and she, too, married young. I was her first–born. I loved going to my grandparents' house because I had uncles and aunts who were close to my age. Uncle John was actually younger than I. While friends complained about having to visit their grandparents because it was boring, I looked forward to those times. We gathered often, usually on Sunday afternoons. It was of one of those Sundays that I had a particularly vivid memory of my grandfather.

The big white box of a farm house was filled with relatives. The women visited in the parlor; the men huddled around the table in the living room, playing cards. Cousins were running helter skelter throughout. At ten, I was torn between spending time with my cousins and spending time with my aunts. After singing songs with Aunt Joan as she played the piano, I decided to check out activities elsewhere. The parlor and the living room were next to each other. I stood in the doorway, mesmerized by the goings on in the living room. The room was hazy with cigarette smoke and it was terribly noisy. The men slapped their hands on the table, drinking beer and laughing as they played poker. After a bit, I noticed that Grandpa wasn't playing. He was off by himself, sitting in the mission oak rocker by the black heating stove. One pink–faced, baby cousin slept on his shoulder, a toddler sat on his lap as he rocked slowly, back and forth. In all that noise and smoke, I watched as in a cloud of unknowing, feeling that somehow the only real people in that room were he, his babies and I.

Keep going, my teacher encourages. Delve deeper.

It was early morning and I was helping Grandma fix breakfast. Rheumatoid arthritis had stiffened her joints. She walked with slow, short steps, like a mechanical doll with worn-down batteries. Every few minutes or so she'd shuffle over to the upstairs steps and shout at Uncle John to get up. Finally, she sent me up to wake him.

They're milking, I said, Come on. They need you.

He pulled the covers over his head. I tugged at his shoulder. He shook me off, grumped at me and rolled over. I went downstairs and told Grandma it was useless. She stood by the window, looking out towards the milk barn. Before long, she shuffled back to the stairs and shouted at John again. He didn't answer. Then Grandpa appeared. He stomped into the house, slamming doors, swearing.

Calm down, Arnie, she said. He's only a child.

The cold angered look on Grandpa's face made me shiver. I slipped behind the table as he tore up the stairs. The sound of flesh against flesh, the thud, the screaming. I felt like vomiting. Sneaking out of the kitchen, I escaped onto the screened front porch. I sat in an old wicker chair and hugged my knees close to my chest, trying to keep my heart from bursting through. I didn't hear Grandpa come down the stairs, but I heard him in the kitchen.

Why does he make me do this? he asked. He walked through the porch without noticing me.

Then John came, trudging down the stairs, slamming, banging, kicking at things in his way. His face was red, he'd been crying. He didn't seem to notice me either. The screen door banged behind him and the fury began all over again. I stood, trembling, too scared to move.

Old bastard! John screamed as he charged at Grandpa like an angry bull calf.

Grandpa knocked him to the ground with his fist. You son of a bitch!

Stop it! I tried to shout. But the words were little more than a whimper.

John lay on the ground, curled up, groaning loudly. Grandpa looked at him a moment, turned and walked away. As John got up and started yelling again, I stood stone–still, sure that this time they'd kill each other. But Grandpa kept walking, slouched and slow, as John stomped and screamed about him. Finally, they disappeared into the barn. I looked at Grandma. She was standing in the kitchen by the sink, crying silently. I crept to the furthest corner of the porch and sobbed. After a while, she found me, told me not to worry, to finish setting the table.

Later, Grandpa came in for breakfast. He sat down at the big trestle table in the kitchen. Grandma busied herself at the stove, mixing a raw egg with the coffee grounds as she poured it into the blue and white speckled coffee pot of boiling water. I sat opposite him, on the bench, thinking about everything. Thinking about how worn out he looked. Thinking about John. The room smelled of morning, of bacon, eggs and fresh brewed coffee. Grandpa filled his cup about three fourths full of the dark brew, then filled it to the rim with thick cream. After stirring it with a spoon, he poured it into his saucer, a little at a time, to cool. He glanced at me. I like my coffee blowed, he said.

Class is over. As I put down my pen, I wonder about prayer. I haven't prayed for a long time. Who should I pray to? As I listen to the splattering rain, I realize that I still think of God like I thought of Him when I was a small child, an old man, all knowing, all powerful. Suddenly, my anger seems as useless and as out of place as that childish image. I need a new vision to help me deal with Christine's illness and the memories of Grandpa, with the suffering, with the helplessness I felt then and feel now. Maybe, I think, God is an old woman, standing by the kitchen sink, crying silent tears. I feel suddenly glad that the rain continues to fall, that fat swirling flakes will not slow my journey home.

Alice Crane

YOUR HANDS

Your hands, now cramped, arthritic
the pain of carpal tunnel syndrome always there, you say
like a nail being driven in from wrist to elbow, like crucifixion.

Hands that pitted cherries
        shelled peas
        fluted crust
        cut corn
        trimmed hair
        stitched clothes
        painted oils
        wove baskets
        wrote poems

Same hands that leapt
        fast as a cobra
        to strike my face
        at the supper table
        night after night
        all the years of my childhood

Until I told you, at 17
I would break those hands
if you ever hit me again.

      Your hands, Mother,
      your hands. I will start by forgiving them.

YOUR BRIGHT BIRD'S EYE

Mother, I cannot forgive
but I release you, wounded jay,
your pain, the infernal squawking
of our intertwined hate.

I have turned my eyeballs inside out
looking backwards,
wrung out my soul for all to see,
descended to the seventh circle
seeking bits
of crystal, gold,
cold, hard cash
among the shit,
your bright bird's eye
always with me.

And I want you to go now,
Mother, I want to forget,
I want to turn my eyes ahead
and look at you now,
I want to see the mother I have now.
I want to see my mother.

Jeanne Bryner

CANDLES

I have come to the house of my childhood to stop wildfires.
Carrying a cool bucket and brush, I prepare to
scrub bloodstains from squeaky doors. The feet
of five children scurry across cold linoleum
floors like rats inside rafters.
Hunger claws at their bellies; I have brought
white milk and yellow cheese to feed
these gray children.

Mama, I beg you to leave the opal heavens long enough to help
me. My blue-eyed husband sleeps warm beside me
in our pine poster bed; my freckled daughter
dreams down the soft carpet hall. This
is the long night, even the wind
is wounded, mama, help me carry the candles.

The candles float in every salty cell of my body. We must try
to put out the fire. Look, mama, here are the candles;
I had to light them for my brothers and sisters,
else they would never believe in the sun.

Seven-hundred-fifty candles for every day of summer
my brothers did not feel damp grass against
their soles, or splash of blue water
press their thighs, or kite string zipping
through their curled fingers. Five summers,
mama, father's witch wife kept them
in the shirt pocket bedroom,
wax-faced and hollow-eyed, and looking out
dirty screen windows, wondering
what it would be like to ride a swing
or bat a ball. Hearing July laughter like a razor
cutting their throats from the neighbor kids
down the street.

There are fifteen hundred candles burning for those stolen
sweet pea summers, mama, summers that can
never be given back. We must take them,
each one of them; we must carry the candles.

Mama, I have one hundred blood red candles burning for my
blonde-haired sister with the inside-out purple eye
and bleeding ears; I had to light a candle
for every single blow. Mama,
I'm sure there were a hundred and her right
breast, swollen, green, red, purple,
and firm as a melon; the candles
were to ease her pain. I have carried
them all these years,
mama, for the August night of her screams
and father's fists and her near death.
Here, help me hold the candles.

Mama, I have two-hundred and seventy candles burning for
the nine months my brunette sister
walked with eyes down because
she was sixteen and pregnant. It was 1965
and no one knew she was starving; her belly
tight as a pale African moon.
Her baby beat a drum of life inside her child's body.
All the pink candles are burning like a birthday
celebration for your first grandchild, mama.

This night we must go to the brown project house, where a
child's rape was kicked under the bed like soiled
underwear. I have come to show you all the
candles burning in my hands, mama.
Father took me to his bed and ruptured me.
I want so much to put out this crackling, dried
limb fire. Mama, see the flames ready
to lick my palms. All the candles are so heavy.

Mama, I have a thousand yellow candles burning for every time
father struck you and choked you blue and
told you you were crazy. Mama, you were never

crazy; you were weary from five children
stacked like blankets over your face, smothering you
season upon season. Nothing to wait for but
our lips at your breasts. Mama, I am pulling
a thousand candles in the wagon,
slowly up autumn's hill; we must try to stop the fire.

My husband turns over in the meadow of his dreams;
my daughter winds her dolly's auburn hair.
Mama, help me in this journey,
my longest, darkest night.

On the ragged steps of the crumpled house, help me carry
in the candles. I do not care that
Mrs. Thompson watches us.
Shall we use our simple tears to stop the fire? Hear
the cries, mama, splitting the tiny house,
everyone here is still crying.
We are coming; we are trying to stop the fire..

Hand me the funnel can, mama. We must finish the task
tonight. Give it to me, mama; please hold
my hand. See how your heavenly match makes it
all burn so fast, so red? Dirty summer screens,
bloody handprints, children running,
warm at last, burning, burning, burning.

Daisy sheets and gasoline sweat beads trickling
from my every pore and scorched flesh stench
bandage wrapped around my ten fingers,
braided through my chestnut hair. Beside me,
my sweet husband sleeping these twenty years
and never fearing this,
his burning wife.

Eve Powers

THE WOMAN AND THE WALL

A woman lives inside a wall. The wall is a circle encompassing her. The wall was begun during the war, by a child. This child grew as the wall grew, and became the woman. This woman-child knows every stone in the wall, remembers placing each one in a particular place, to prevent the repetition of a specific injury. Eventually, the wall became a kind of tomb, enclosing the woman completely, and inside there was a loneliness like death.

For a long time, it was dark inside the wall. The woman was haunted by nightmares about the war, and sometimes she could not tell whether she was still in the war, or only remembering it.

One day, there was a very slight shift in some of the ceiling stones. A crack appeared, and for an instant through that crack a brilliant light flashed down. Somehow, the woman knew that the light came from Christ, or perhaps even was Christ. After this, events of richness, subtlety and beauty occurred within the wall, and the terrible loneliness was driven away.

Lately, however, the woman has had a recurring nightmare. She sees clean, pale beige sand, close up, as if bending down to inspect a beach. On this sand is a low circle of sand, about an inch high. As the woman watches, clear water, the farthest edge of an incoming wave, gently and silently washes through the small barrier and innundates the circle. She wakes with a feeling of horror. She is thirsty and feels she cannot get enough air.

Now, even during the day, the feelings that follow the nightmare are becoming stronger. Something is growing inside her, and as it grows, she notices with alarm that the stones in the wall are somehow becoming smaller. Cracks are appearing between the stones even as a howl grows in the woman. She knows that this howl cannot be expressed inside the wall, so she begins, terrified, to loosen some of the stones. Part of her screams, "Stop! Rebuild the wall before it is too late!" She prays to the light for courage. She feels smothered and must get out. She feels that to go out would be the worst betrayal of herself.

Suddenly, the wall begins to crumble and the woman cannot stop it. She finds herself on a hill, standing within a circle of stones, looking out at a world ignorant of her war.

The woman breathes, listens, hears only birds, sees a hawk circling. The trees are leafless, the ground gray with dead grass and leaves. Below her, a field is shockingly green with early wheat, and she can see the distant silver thread of a river. It is not spring yet, but spring cannot be far away. A few raindrops patter on the dead leaves just as the sun breaks free of the black clouds, catching the woman in a ray of light.

The unbearable howl that has been growing inside her begins to pour out. At first it is just a sound, a long, repeated scream of outrage. After a long time, the sound becomes a single anguished word howled over and over again: "I.........!" "I.........!" "I.........!"

The woman feels that she could howl forever. It is the story of her war, her story of herself.

Jane Orleman

MY LIFE AS AN ARTIST

Since the sixteenth century art has been an effective and valuable means to explore and communicate social and spiritual crisis. Nevertheless, it was not until the twentieth century that the feminine crisis of the soul began to be examined in the visual arts. The life experiences addressed in this volume are not new to our generation but we are the first to speak of them openly on the world stage.

The paintings included in this essay speak of violation, emotional, physical and sexual, specifically within the home. They depict the experience and its effects in later life. The viewpoint is that of the female child. However, the grief, despair and pain inflicted on the souls of the victims, survivors, perpetrators and the family members affect us all, and they are handed down from parent to child for generations. Often their effects are so hidden that many of us who have been actively entangled seem to be unaware of them. In fact, earlier in this century it was considered acceptable in this country for a man to beat his wife and children. The masculine and feminine aspects of our society have been out of balance for a long time, resulting in crimes against the souls of women. The first step in stopping the crimes against women and our children is to acknowledge them. With that in mind, I offer you my story.

At 27 years of age, I had been drifting in and out of college for nine years. I had attended five universities in the Northeast, South and Western United States, always changing majors, yearning for meaningful occupation. When I came to Central Washington University as a senior, it was to study geography, a reasonable choice for someone seeking direction. I loved to draw maps.

Soon after arriving, a friend took me through the art department. He said, "You can make art. You need to make art." I began with stick figures. I knew then that I had found my life's work. That was twenty-five years ago.

I changed majors for the last time and enjoyed three absorbing years completing a BA in art. For the next eight years, I painted interiors in an effort to learn my craft by rendering the world around me. Then I returned to the major inspiration from my college years, a need to express my sexuality in spiritual terms. This work spanned the next eight years. In retrospect, I see that both of these directions set the stage for my current work. The interiors created the foundation for the recent work in the "child voice." They also created grounding or a sense of safety which I desperately needed. I spent hundreds of hours painting my home with flowers on the table, the dog in a chair, everything in its place. There was never any overturned furniture, no signs of a struggle. For many years there were no people. Gradually, my husband and I came into the picture. As soon as people arrived, so did sexual content. My safety began to slip away.

It wasn't only in my art that I had attempted to create a distance between me and the world. I had been playing hide and seek with my past for a long time, using drugs, alcohol and miles to protect me. Having put 3,000 miles between me and my parents for a dozen years, I was totally unprepared when they came for a visit and decided to stay. Within three days they had bought a house. Thus began five years of desperately trying to please them and hating myself for doing it. For three of those years I saw a therapist weekly in an effort to cope with my out of control emotions.

That was when I returned to the earlier painting style and imagery, trying to put the sexuality into a spiritual context. I was unconsciously taking my sexual conflict and projecting it to a cosmic setting thousands of miles into the stars. Working with the sexual material in this way allowed me to create a safe distance from which to relate to the most horrifying experiences of my life. This cooler style has become what I call the "symbolic voice" in my more recent work. Images that center me and speak of completeness are painted in this style.

After eight years of distancing my inner demons, I began to experience a creative block. For the next few years I painted portraits just to keep my skills alive and growing. But I knew there was a creative crisis brewing. I found it increasingly difficult to face my studio. My parents had left after five years at my insistence. At the time I knew that guilt was going to be my great enemy. There was an obvious danger of being overwhelmed by guilt for driving them away. By being aware and vigilant, I was able to keep guilt at bay for several years. However it was done at the expense of having to shut down thoughts and emotions to the point of becoming a vacuum. I was spending my time playing endless games of solitaire, reading science fiction and smoking cigarettes.

I think now that the art I needed to do was art that I was not yet ready to do. I had to become desperate to work before I would be willing to paint the images which lived inside me. It was an event in the outer world which brought the inner crisis to my conscious attention. My mother died in the crash of a small plane. She was on her way to visit me. As far as I could tell, my mother disapproved of my artwork. When she came to visit I usually agonized over which paintings to hide away. Perhaps my perception of her disapproval was a projection of my own self condemnation. But whatever is the case, I am sure I couldn't have painted these images from my childhood if she was here to see them.

However, on the surface, it was the renewed awareness of my mortality which caught my attention. Life is short. I needed to use my time here to do my work; enjoy my life, my garden, my home, my body; to share the fullness of all my experiences with my husband, but in fact, I had shut out the world in an attempt to keep painful emotions from overwhelming me. I was so successful that I didn't know **why** I had narrowed my life to two chairs, a deck of cards, a stack of books and my smokes.

Smoking was making me sick. If I continued, life would be short and miserable. I had tried to quit many times in the past thirty-five years but it was the only socially acceptable form of suicide left to me, a way to express my self hatred. Now it was time to make a choice for life. This choice led me to a clinical psychologist who would occasionally use hypnosis to help a smoker quit the habit, but he often turned away that type of client as too boring. His stop smoking program was a seven hour package deal. In the first two-hour session, I quit. There I was with five paid-up hours of therapy. So I said, "Maybe you can help me with this other little problem, a creative block."

I had hoped for the same kind of magic—quit smoking—start painting. It wasn't that easy. In an early session, Dr. W. introduced me to a breathing exercise similar to the type of breathing used in childbirth. I don't know what his expectations were, but it provoked a tremendously deep response from within me. I cried out in pain, sobbed and felt great fear. This was incredible to me as I am usually very self contained. He assured me that I could stop this experience at any moment. However, I realized that if my response was this powerful it was too important to leave unfinished. He asked me what past experience these feelings evoked. I said, "The Rape."

"How old are you?"

"Eleven."

"Who is there?"

"My brother. His friends."

Through the intensity of this experience I realized that the past still held me imprisoned. My fear had frozen my feelings. I have never forgotten the events. They had been stored safely away. Now, like Pandora, I had just opened the box.

In the following week, I wrote down many of my painful secrets, a childhood biography. I took the pages to the next therapy session. Handing them to Dr. W., I said, "There, now you know what happened. I don't want to talk about it." Later in going through a box of stuff, I came across a similar document that I had written for the therapist ten years ago when dealing with my parents' return to my life.

By now I was two months into the therapy process and had done only one or two unfinished paintings. Dr. W. dropped a stone into these still waters. He asked, "Have you ever painted from your own life experiences?" I resisted the idea at first, and he said, "What else do you have?" The logic of it struck me, of course, this is the life I have been given. To ignore it as a source is to deny my life.

So I began this visual dialogue between me and myself, my present and my past, me and my therapist. Once I accepted this journey, I gave myself a set of guidelines. Never censor the creative process. Trust the expressions of my thoughts and feelings as they appear in the paintings. Always share the work and be honest with Dr. W. Do the work necessary to face my demons and to follow where the path leads me. I thought that I had already dealt with my childhood experience. It hadn't worked. This time I was committed to truly doing the work and then doing it again.

I started with one or two paintings a month. Their images were inspired by subjects discussed in therapy sessions. After nine months of working with Dr. W., he proposed that I devote an afternoon to thinking, feeling or acting like a child. That suggestion led to a series of small paintings from the point of view of myself as a child. These images in the child's voice allowed me to say in paint what I found so difficult to say in words. I have always been a skeptic about the inner child, but by allowing the child a voice the dam exploded and the creative block was broken. Soon I was doing six to eight paintings a month instead of one or two. About one third of these were in the child's voice. The rest reflected my feelings as an adult about the painful events in my past and about the process of revealing and accepting those events. As I progressed a third painting voice appeared, one to express strong emotion. I attribute the development of this "emotional voice" to Dr. W's sustained efforts to introduce me to my inner masculine. It was a concept that I resisted vigorously. I believe now that the acceptance of that masculine energy opened the doorway to the intense creative drive which had been missing in my life. The first of the emotional voice images resulted from the suggestion to spend an afternoon in a masculine experience mode. So, I decided to paint like a man which to my way of thinking was big and sloppy. In the four years that my emotional center and life experiences have been the creative source for the artwork, I have painted more than I had in the previous twenty years. There are nearly three hundred images in this series.

Opening to this material was by no means easy. One of the things that made it possible is seen when viewing the paintings in their entirety. Interspersed throughout the work are "safety paintings." Some are mandalas which create a sheltered place within, others are images of safe retreats. Invariably, such a protecting image would precede deeper revelations containing heavy emotional impact. They are like diving boards to the unconscious.

In reviewing the body of work, the evolutionary nature of therapy became visible. In the first rendition of the gang rape, I was a stick figure with a black void in place of a head. During the next four years I was able to re-experience some of the anguish, pain and fear of that rape. It became important to me to get as close as possible to the emotional reality of that soul searing experience. Since trying to forget my childhood traumas hadn't worked, I decided to remember them and to interact with those memories. I thought perhaps the acceptance of that reality could rechannel the power it held over my life.

The three painting voices also appear throughout the work as aspects of myself; the angry self, the hidden self and the self who acts in the world. In 1990, these aspects exhibited degrees of separation, hostility and unawareness of one another. By 1993 they had an inner and outer awareness that allowed them to name themselves and stand united. I speak of them as characters in an inner drama but they also have an outer reality as they interact through me with the world. In the process of blending these and other attributes, I have been able to create the paintings, aggressively seek exhibitions, and to speak publicly about the work. Looking through the images, I see these and many other aspects of myself which have helped revitalize my view of the world. I do not view these characters as evidence of multiple personalities, but as a means of symbolic self portrayal. They give me a frame of reference which allows me to expand who I am.

These characters are by no means clearly defined. They weave into one another and evolve through time. There are very strong connections between my angry self, the masculine force, and the beast within. The masculine models available to me as a child had been raging, unpredictable and cruel. Consequently I depict the masculine force as a wild beast who later became an inner monster, my Homicidal Maniac. Once he was revealed within me, through the paintings, I set out to embrace that part of myself, which I had previously feared and rejected. The monster is still there but my relationship to it has changed.

The same shifting nature is seen with other symbols, such as the skeleton figure. Early in the work it represents the perpetrator of overwhelming sexual assault and, later, the connection to the lost soul. Both the monster and the skeleton which symbolize my deepest fears eventually evolved to depict hidden strengths, as well.

My earliest memories are of being molested. Between the years of three and eight this happened often. Between the ages of nine and thirteen I was subject to almost daily emotional, physical or sexual assault. Rarely did a day go by without violence in our home. I passed my teenage years in a drug and alcohol daze. Until recently, I had adopted the attitude that this had all happened in a long dead past. Now, I realize painting these images has helped me accept the events which shaped my view of myself and the world for the past forty years.

However, I seldom set out to paint a particular event. The image comes to me as I paint. I consider my paintings a dialogue with myself. I approach the canvas with thoughts brought up in the therapeutic process. For instance, I might sit for a few minutes before I start an image and ask myself "why is it so hard for me to express anger?" That question resulted in the image titled "Daddy Enraged." The painting process results from my deeper self telling me what I feel, think, or sometimes, remember. Very often these are feelings and thoughts of which I am not consciously aware. Openness to this inner dialogue has created the visual evidence detailing a journey of self discovery.

I paint with oils, using a fast drying medium which I discovered when I began this body of work. The first decision to be made about a painting is the size. Sometimes I know immediately which canvas to use, other times I might handle a half a dozen before one feels correct. The child voice is usually a small one, the emotional voice can be quite large. However, the reverse has also been true. It has been important to me to keep open to surprise, to not become the director but let the images flow. At first, I applied the paint with small sable brushes. As the "emotional voice" became more active, I had a dream which led me into using large palette knives. Soon after, at Dr. W's suggestion, I took up a butcher knife as my primary painting instrument. When I returned to brushes, it was the oversized variety that drew my interest. Now I am apt to use all of these tools on a single painting. I find that I have options in my art and in my life that I didn't have before I began this work.

Outside of my art, the most amazing of these new options has been the decision to get a driver's license. After thirty-five years of being afraid to drive, I suddenly decided that I could do it. I hadn't been aware of driving as a desire nor even conscious of its loss. I had believed that it was beyond my abilities for so long that I rarely thought about it at all. But one day I found myself looking at cars on the highway and thinking about what features I would like in my car, and the desire crystalized. A month later I had a car and a license. Such a bold pursuit. It's been nearly a year and I still shake my head in amazement that I can drive across town or across three states.

In my art, the new options have taken a variety of forms. Among them, the creation of images which deal with the process of therapy and the therapeutic relationship, as I do in the painting "Getting Out the Poison." There are a number of obstacles to both the process and relationship which my work tries to overcome. We are taught, for example, that it's not acceptable to talk about ourselves, to dominate a conversation or to tell our secrets. In therapy, we do all of these things; we reveal everything to a stranger. We are called upon to trust another person, and in my case, a man. Sometimes it is necessary to get angry, project the anger onto the therapist and still keep working with him. There were times in my own process when my therapist seemed to not understand me and times when he understood me too well. But, the deal we made was that he was willing to work with me as long as I was willing to work. Once I realized that the past was still alive, I knew that I would need the help of someone who understood emotional and psychological reality as well as physical reality. I am very appreciative of the fact that he and so many others in the mental health field are there to support those of us who feel the need to make sense of our lives.

At the same time that I discovered art, twenty-five years ago, I began a dream journal. The number of dreams recorded has paralleled the number of paintings; two hundred in the first 20 years and three hundred in the next five. Once I showed a willingness to listen, my unconscious has had a great deal to say to me. The paintings have restated dream images and vice versa. The interconnections of the dreams and images are not always readily apparent to me. Again, it is the process of viewing the art and dreams in retrospect which has brought glimmers of enlightenment.

As I exhibit, give slide shows, and write about my work I gain a fuller understanding of its meaning. Often, it is the viewer who reflects back to me deeper insights on a particular image. I have been amazed and moved by the responses to the exhibits, which have been used by communities and on university campuses to create an awareness of this emotional wound which devastates our society. These paintings are intensely personal. Unfortunately, however, my experiences are not unique. Child molestation and rape are not uncommon, physical violence towards children is a daily occurrence around the globe. In recent years, art shows, plays, movies and books have begun to express this reality. The resulting discussions help to free others to face their secrets. Our secrets can become monsters, consuming energy to keep the truth hidden from ourselves and the world long after the original insult is past. Eventually the monster within does gnaw its way out. It often takes thirty or forty years to free itself, bursting upon the world in a fit of murderous madness or an incredible flood of creativity. Truth telling does not get rid of the beast but it will begin to change our relationship with the monster and its effect on us all.

On the following pages there is a sequence of paintings by Jane Orleman.

BAD GIRL

DAMNED DADDY

BEYOND ALL REASON

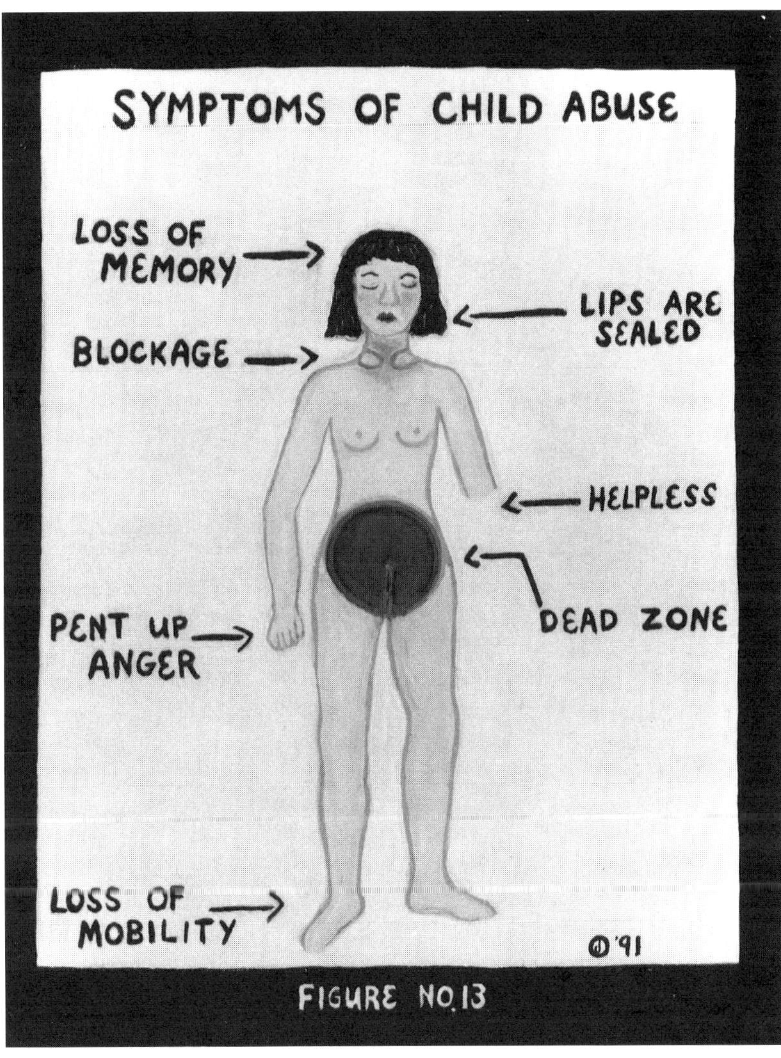

SYMPTOMS OF CHILD ABUSE

SURROUNDED BY AN UNKNOWN FEAR

IF LOOKS COULD KILL

Jeff Walt

RUINS

I was there with you when you turned five
unable to ride a bicycle
like your sister did at that age,
training wheels until you were seven,
playing with matches,
dressing in girls' clothes,
applying make-up to your
eyes and cheekbones, a gypsy:
you prayed for a vagina, wished
upon stars until they
freckled the sky.

At nine, neighbors had you drunk
and dancing naked on the kitchen tale.
Disco music became air
that you inhaled—unable to live
without it—while someone flashed
the kitchen light off and on,
until you were too tired
and someone older
carried you off like an infant
to the bedroom up the stairs
and down the hall: where each took
a turn teaching you, as they said,
to love.

When ten years of life
spilled into your body,
you were seduced
by a forty-four-year old man
who thought he'd try
and score with your mother.
Drunk that night, passed out,
she talked to herself in the next room
while you licked the genitals
of a stranger: hairier
and bigger than yourself.

Twenty years have brought you here:
sitting complacent, a leather chair
molding beneath you, the smell
of violets coming from somewhere,
explaining guilt to Dr. Puckett;
you wanted the sex, even then, to fill
the empty bivouac of your heart.
And I was there with you,
because you reside in me:
dressed in knee-torn jeans,
red face, balancing in railroad tracks,
arms extended, not even slipping off.
They all want to touch you, but they can't,
now that I won't allow it.

SOLACE, LATE IN THE DAY

for Jason Stuart

Today I loved my dog's sour breath.
His tongue entered my mouth
by accident and it wasn't so bad.
I loved the smell of radish
under my fingernails
and the headless Barbie Doll
a child must've buried in my garden.
I know I can never have children
because history repeats itself.
I love my muffler that drags
and the holes in my underwear,
the way my skin wrinkles
around my eyes when I smile,
and my sore hip that gives away my age.
I love this damp house
that smells of Windex and Pledge;
how I carefully smoothed the fine mahogany
of the coffee table; held the knobbed spine
of the rocker the way I did my first lover
with so much precision.
I know I cannot bring back the dog
my brother and I skinned alive.
I loved the bath water that went cold
this afternoon as the last slab
of pink broke from the sky like slate
as God crawled onto the windowsill
with the breeze and watched me dry off.
He came to me without a penis or foreplay,
without saying good-bye. He left me
with my life around me and I kept it.

IT'S YOUR LIFE AND YOU CAN LAUGH IF YOU WANT TO

"It's never too late to have a happy childhood."
— Tom Robbins

Chances are, if you and I were in the same room right now, we'd both be laughing. I am a freelance humor writer and stand-up comic, so laughing and making people laugh is part of my job. I'm also a human being, and I've found that laughter is the best way to survive whatever life decides to throw at me.

I discovered the miracle of laughter late in life. According to my mother, as a toddler I spent far more time in tears than in smiles. As a teen, Edgar Allen Poe and Sylvia Plath were my favorite companions. Even in early adulthood, I took life more seriously than most. I recently spoke with my old first college roommate with whom I hadn't kept in touch. She was stunned at the change in me. During our conversation, she asked at least three times, "You *are* the Leigh Anne I lived with for two years, right?"

Certainly my childhood and early adult years do not seem to be the stuff of which comedy is made. In my father's house, we were just as likely to end up spending an evening rushing my stepmother to the hospital after yet another suicide attempt as we were to sit down to a quiet supper. I remember that when our house was put on the market, we had to spackle in bullet holes in the walls and buy new bedroom doors to replace those that had been beaten in. Like so many young women in this situation, I escaped by marrying a man who carried on the abuse—only this time it was verbal and emotional—leaving no bruises, only psychological scars.

Now I am 37 and I laugh a lot. I laugh with my new spouse, our two wiener dogs, and our friends. I laugh because I've lived long enough now to know that laughing really is the best survival tool we humans have. You know those stories you read in the newspaper about people who are stranded for weeks at sea or lost in the woods and when they are rescued, dehydrated and starving, they still have their sense of humor intact? It's not at all ironic that they can still see the humor in life. Seeing humor is what kept them alive. Even in the horror of Nazi concentration camps, people survived because of their ability to transcend the reality of daily life by finding humor. I keep this in mind whenever I start to take my life too seriously.

So instead of dwelling on the past to see if there's any horror I've repressed that I could dredge up and feel more miserable about, I MAKE FUN. That is the way humor works when we use it to heal ourselves. For example, in my stand-up act, I say: "My step-mother slit her wrists so often her arms were six inches shorter than when she married my dad. She always had one wrist wrapped in a bloody bandage. She looked like a giant tampon."

If You Can't See The Bright Side - Polish The Dull Side!

Of course I didn't go from glum twentysomething to jovial thirtysomething overnight. There were lots of steps—big and small.

The biggest step was getting divorced. There is absolutely no doubt that divorce was one of the best things that ever happened to me. I divorced not only my verbally abusive spouse, but also all the childhood insecurities that made me stay in the relationship so long. I guess you could say I divorced my childhood—I agreed to put it behind me and let it be part of my past. I let go of my father's extreme disappointment that I had been born a girl and his efforts to pretend I was a boy. I let go of my father's refusal to let me cry because it didn't accomplish anything. I let go of the guilt of not having been physically abused myself when my siblings were (I was "the favorite"). I let go of the fact that in between mothers, I had devoted most of my childhood to raising my brothers and sisters.

Then there was therapy. I went for four sessions. The entire first hour was spent crying. How the therapist understood anything I said is beyond me. I told him somewhere in that first session that my father never let me cry and my husband never let me laugh (he actually said on numerous occasions, "Intelligent people don't laugh out loud!" and I was stupid enough or cowed enough to believe him!) The second therapy session, I distinctly remember saying, "I've never had any fun in my life!" By the third session, I decided that the pursuit of fun was absolutely essential for getting on with my life and making up for not having a childhood. By my final session I had a plan for making friends and trying things I'd never done with the narrow goal of having as much fun as I could.

I started reading funny books-Art Buchwald, Dave Barry, Cathy Guisewaite, Berkeley Breathed, and so forth. I went to funny moves. I even went to see a comedian (by myself—a first!). I sat all alone in my empty house watching sitcoms on television and laughing out loud and not noticing any decline in my intellectual capacity.

And then something funny happened. I talked to my mom. In the course of our adult lives, my mom and I had only talked at length a few times. After all, she was in and out of marriages and not always mentally stable. I thought she was part of my problem—I had always blamed her for "leaving us" with my dad, even though I knew she hadn't really had a choice. Well, one day after my divorce, she called. We talked. I listened. What I heard was funny. My mom made me laugh. And, as it turned out, I made her laugh too. This simple conversation opened many doors. I thought to myself, "I have laughter in my genes!" (I had always known I had gotten "dancing" genes from her, but hadn't realized the "laughing" genes had been there). Then, I thought, "Hey, if she can laugh through her life which has been even more challenging than mine, I can laugh too!"

Another important thing that happened during this period of time that helped bring laughter into my life was that I became chair of a volunteer committee for the American Heart Association. Having just divorced myself from the rest of my life and now being in a leadership role with a group of people who didn't know me too well, I had a chance to reinvent myself. I tried to be funny. I made our meetings fun. I dressed in neon colors (as opposed to the grays and browns that had been the main components of my wardrobes for decades). I threw really great volunteer thank you parties that everyone talked about for months. Our group got so much accomplished that the national association used a lot of the ideas we developed. And, we had such a reputation for being loud and silly that at annual meetings, we were always seated at the back (we were far too disruptive!). From this I learned that being silly and funny can actually make work and relationships more successful. It forced me to re-examine my approach to being a "serious professional."

So, little by little, laughter and fun were taking over my life. People started calling me just to chat because they knew I could make them laugh and relieve their stress. As a wellness professional at the time, stress management was one of the things that was part of my job responsibilities, and I loved having a tool that really seemed to work.

Then, in spring of 1992, I was working with a volunteer committee at work to try to put together an activity to lower stress among employees as part of Mental Health Month (May). We decided (at my insistence) to perform comedy sketches based on Saturday Night Live characters for departments that won the "We're

Under the Most Stress!" contest. I ended up having to write the sketches as well as be one of the lead performers. It was great fun and still is remembered as one of the best things we ever did for employees.

But having to write funny was a whole new experience for me. I could be funny extemporaneously, but found it very hard to put it in writing. So, in my continuing quest for adding humor and fun to my life, I signed up for a 4-hour comedy writing class. Which, in turn lead to a 6-week stand-up comedy class. Which lasted for 18 months. And during the time I was in the class, I made friends with absolutely wonderful, funny people, with sad to violent to horrible lives. One of my best friends, a female comic in her late 60s would do comedy about her husband's declining mental abilities and vision, his low opinion of her intelligence, her 40-ish son who had moved back in with her with his child, and her struggle to support them all and stay sane. She'd start off, "My family said 'Don't you even think about trying to go out somewhere tonight and do comedy. You're not funny!' But, I untied the knots with my teeth, thanks to Poligrip, and here I am!" This woman continues to inspire me even though I have moved across country.

Now I teach my own class. For people who want to write or perform comedy, or who need comedy therapy. I hope I can give back to them some of what others gave me—laughter, fun, and life!

Today, I look at everything as possibly comedic. I read the papers trying to find funny material in the headlines and stories. I repeat over and over to myself a statement I read in the New York Times several years ago, "There is absolutely not one shred of scientific evidence that life is serious!" I have a well-stocked humor library of my own that I lend out to anyone in need. My spouse and I watch funny movies and TV shows together. And I teach and perform comedy—all of it based upon my life and how I view the world through humor-colored glasses.

Be Serious!

I believe we've all been victims of violence—either directly or indirectly. And at some point, most of us try to help someone else who is a victim. But when it comes to violence, most people think that laughter is out-of-place, inappropriate, and trivializing. Perhaps even hurtful. After all, serious situations call for serious attitudes, right? And the only attitudes that seem acceptable in violent situations appear to be denial, anger, sadness, and acceptance—

much the same as those emotions accepted as part of the grieving process. From the first time we are told, "Be serious! This isn't funny!," we understand society's message that laughter is childish and disdained. Is it any wonder that the average American child laughs out loud 300 times a day and the average American adult laughs only fifteen?

We react to death and violence in the same ways. But there is one major difference—at least death gets it over with. The end comes. You grieve, you move on. With violence, every day there is anger, fear, and stress. We all feel the damage from these emotions—stomach tied in knots, ulcers, muscle tension and fatigue, TMJ, high blood pressure, difficulty breathing, gastrointestinal distress, etc. Add to this the daily stresses that are part of everyone's life and it's a wonder any of us survive from day to day, if we are in abusive situations.

On the other hand, laughter, that "unacceptable" response to trauma and crisis, is itself healing. A simple test is to ask yourself how your body feels when you laugh as compared to when you get angry. It feels good! And it feels good, because with each laugh, physiological processes are occurring that renew and revive. When you laugh, your body releases endorphins, naturally produced pain-killing hormones that serve to help combat headache, backache, muscle ache, and other physical pain. Laughing also causes the body to produce an enzyme that helps coat your stomach and protect it from excess acid, thus reducing ulcers and stomach problems. The laughing process lowers blood pressure and heart rate for several hours. Recent research indicates that laughing also strengthens the immune system by reducing the amount of serotonin produced in response to stressful situations.

Laughing also increases the circulation of blood and oxygen to all major organs, including your brain. This results in clearer thinking, improved decision-making, and a better ability to resolve conflicts. Deep belly-laughing exercises all your major muscle groups. One minute of belly-laughing gives you the same abdominal exercise as 25 sit-ups!

One of the most important benefits of laughter is that a good sense of humor helps put things in perspective. A good laugh is like a mini-vacation from your problems. It also makes you feel like you have more control over your life. Because when you **choose** to laugh, you **choose** something that is good for mind, body, and soul.

"So Oftentimes It Happens That We Live Our Life in Chains and We Never Even Know We Have the Key"— The Eagles

Personal violence and abuse are not funny. Millions of women, children, seniors, and men suffer ever year. But even when you are caught in the middle of violence yourself, there are aspects of your life in which humor is present. Having been there myself, I usually tell people: (1) get out as soon as you can; and (2) choose not to be any more miserable than you have to. Which means, of course, choose to find humor where it does exist - movies, books, friends, children, pets, work, ...

Steve Allen said "Comedy equals tragedy plus time." And for most of us, we eventually look back at the traumas of our lives and find some humor. Brett Butler, star of the TV program "Grace Under Fire," has taken her tragedy of life with an abusive husband and shared her humor with us. "I wasn't married to a redneck. I was married to a subliterate, terra-cotta-toothed imbecile with violent tendencies. In other words, he's a simian knuckleheaded dragon, trailer-dwelling amoebae. That may sound mean, but he doesn't understand."

If you listen closely to most comics (at least those whose language is clean enough sit through), you will note the darkness of their topics. Alcoholism, drug use, broken relationships, abuse, violence, personal tragedy—all are standard fare for comedians. Comedians, by virtue of their occupation, find humor in tragedy almost as quickly as it happens in their lives.

Most of us, however, wait too long to find the humor in our own lives. While we usually eventually laugh at ourselves, we wait so long that in the process we are ourselves responsible for abusing our bodies—with stress, fear, and anger.

With laughter, it is even possible to speed the time between tragedy and comedy. A good friend of mine had lost his 35-year-old brother unexpectedly. After several months of depression following the funeral, he asked me to help him find a way to come to terms with the death. I asked him, point blank, if there was anything funny about the funeral. He said, reluctantly, "Yes." He then told me that the funeral director urged him and his father over to one side of the room in a hushed voice. "We have an emergency," he hissed. My friend replied, "He's dead. How much of an emergency can it be?" After telling this story, a smile broke out across my friend's face. It was if he had been granted permission to laugh again.

I am not suggesting here that we should seek to find humor in violence, abuse, and death. My point is that there is more to all of our lives than violence. What we can all do, regardless of our life circumstances, is actively seek out humor and work to make sure that we are surrounded by things that can make us laugh and feel good. If you are surrounded by things that regularly make you laugh, it becomes easier and more natural to find humor, even in the darker moments of life.

This is a fairly simple task if you approach it logically. Here are some suggestions:

- Seek out people who make you laugh. A good friend who brings you to laughter easily can be as therapeutic as years of counseling.
- Invest in things that make you laugh. My personal supply includes animal snouts, books (Dave Barry has saved the day many times!), buttons (I wish I had worn the one that says "I'm not really listening to you" during my first marriage), calendars, cards, coffee mugs, doormats, music, pencils, post-it-notes, underwear with lobsters.
- Take this idea one step further and create your own humor first aid kit. Put into your kit anything that always brings a smile. The next time you find yourself overly stressed, bring out something from your kit for a quick shot of perspective and a dose of the healing power of humor.
- Add humor to your writing. If you have to write something down—whether it's a letter home, memo to the cafeteria about the cockroach you found in your meatless lasagna, grocery list, note to a friend, note to yourself (Dear Self—where did you put the lid to the toothpaste?)—you can easily make it humorous by putting your message on a funny post-it, notepad, or card.
- If you need to get away from your problems, spend 15 minutes at a card store reading funny cards. It's a cheap way to get control of your emotions.
- And probably the cheapest way to add laughter to your life—just laugh! All those great things that go on inside your body when you laugh don't wait until you feel like laughing. All you have to do in go through the motions to get the benefits of laughter. It's the same principle as exercise—you get the benefits of exercise whether you feel like doing it or not.

If you feel that you are ready to start turning your current tragedies into comedies, there are two other suggestions:

- Write a humor autobiography. In my comedy-writing classes, I have students write a straightforward autobiography, focusing on the events that had the most impact on their lives—positive and negative. We then work together to add humor. Many people take this class purely for its therapeutic value! You can learn how to write simple jokes to make yourself laugh by using a book like Gene Perret's *Comedy Writing Step-by-Step*.

- Keep a humor diary. Every day, write down the things that cause you the most stress. Then try to find something funny. One of the easiest ways to do this is to ask yourself, "How could it have been worse?" An entry might read, "Mom was drunk again when I came home. But at least she wasn't sitting in the middle of the front yard pulling weeds in the nude again!"

When trying to find humor in your life, don't worry about how other people will respond or feel about what you've written. You're doing this for you and as long as you use it privately and therapeutically, it doesn't matter what they might think.

> *"What The People Need is a Way To Make Them Smile"*
> — Doobie Brothers

If your current role is not coping with violence in your own life, but helping someone else cope, you may find it very difficult to reach out to friends and loved ones with humor. Being a funny friend in need can be a frightening prospect because most of us are afraid that our humor might be misinterpreted as lack of concern.

On the other hand, if your relationships are limited by the fact that you feel you can only offer sympathy and tears, you are cheating yourself and your friends out of the healing power of humor. One of the worst things facing individuals in violent situations is that all their relationships focus on violence, anger, and fear. They have too little joy, silliness, and fun.

Here's another real-life example, again dealing with death. The father of a very close friend of mine died after a prolonged bout with lung cancer. Because he had been in the hospital for six months and was given no hope of ever recovering, she had started the grieving process long before his death. Instead of a sympathy card, I sent her a humorous card about friendship. She called two days later and said, "I thought I'd forgotten how to laugh. Thank you for reminding me how good it is!"

The most important thing to remember when trying to use humor to help friends cope with abuse is not to focus on their situation. If they find humor in their circumstances, laugh with them. When you initiate humor, it should come from your own life.

To be that funny friend in need, you can go to funny movies together, rent her favorite comedian on videotape, do something silly together like singing Karaoke, send humorous cards, buy humorous sentiments ("Cheer up! Things are getting worse at a slower rate!" — Ashley Brilliant), call to leave a new joke every day on her answering machine, buy items for his humor first aid kit.... the list is limited only by your own imagination.

Laughter Can Save Your Life

Many of you have read this far and you're certain that you will never be able to laugh, nor should you, at a situation as serious as abuse. For you, I share one last anecdote. There is probably no situation more brutal and demeaning than that faced by American prisoners of war during the Vietnam war. One POW told how he had decided on a certain day that he could not longer tolerate the daily beatings and had planned to end his life. As he entered the shower that morning, he noticed, in letters carved into the wall, the following: "Smile! You're on Candid Camera!" He smiled. In the midst of brutality with no end in sight, he smiled. And he chose to live another day. And another. A few weeks later, the war was over and he was freed.

Laughter can save your life!

Gary Young

To survive his years in solitary confinement, a man invented a castle, and filled it with candles, tapestries, silver and wrought iron. Another man imagined a resort, and spent his days setting tables, fixing menus, making beds. All those years, dreaming of the same house, discovering, every night, another room, a hidden passage, a secret chamber, I never thought of the passing days. I fingered the dark molding along the unexpected corridors, hung curtains or set rafters, until the blows of a hammer, or the blood pounding in my ears, would wake me.

My mother loved violets. When she spent whole days in bed for days on end, I brought her violets, and put them in a cup on the nightstand by her head. I skipped lunch all week for the money to buy them, and the florist would nod, and say, violets again. When I brought them home, my mother said, you precious thing. Then she'd look at the flowers and say, they're beautiful, but they never last.

My cousin had a dream last night about my mother. He said, I was sobbing, and she held me, and rocked me in her arms as I cried. She turned, and looked behind us, at a room full of people, and I asked, do they know you're here? And she said, no, no they don't. My cousin said, I'd never dreamed of her before, and I woke up happy; I was still crying, but I felt all right. Then he stopped, and I asked, how is she? And he said, great, great. She looked great.

Anne Stilwell

MOTHER, MY HISTORY

my mother
small brown bird
fits in the palm of a hand
tossed skyward, dives and swoops
then returns to earth

gave birth
to a raven
loud black and raucous
that gets in your dreams
unsettles

mother
field of daisies
    (simplicity too easy
    look deeper)
tulip petals tight
then opening
the annuals, perennials
weeded beds
my mother the work
of soil into comfort
green spears coaxed
fingers dirty
knuckles hard and bony
giving life

from her body
a rose
thorns drawing blood
weed, thistle, nettle
untame
a nuisance to order
not obeying
the border of bed
or plot
root and thrive
in neighbors' backyards

discomfort and fear
unable to rid
themselves of me
I declare myself
my history

what my mother gave me
through her body, these words
daughter of daughter of daughter
humming through my blood

Patricia Rose Gilles

THERE ARE MANY OF ME

A Personal Story of Healing From Child Abuse

Surviving starts at a very young age when you begin to bury what you see, experience, and feel because the pain is too great. Before I buried the pain, however, I remember trying to first figure out some of the things that didn't make sense to me. Why didn't my mother pray when our whole family did devotions? I remember asking my father if my mother was a Catholic and he was shocked at my question. He didn't realize that to this young mind, not praying with us meant mom was not one of us. How did I come to realize that it was because she couldn't stand the sight of us? When she would say, "Get out of my sight!"? Or when she refused to kiss us good-night turning the other way and saying, "Go to bed." Why did we get our mouths washed out with soap for saying "bad words" but our mother could call us, "Goddamn little shits"? And why were we taught to "turn the other cheek," only to receive facial blows from our own parents?

How could a father who gave the most wonderful hugs, slam small bodies into walls or hit one of us with his fork at the dinner table because we laughed at the wrong time? How could a mother who gave birth to us show such hate, slap our faces and hit us with sticks so hard that they would break? How could a loving grandfather invade private places shaming little bodies barely out of diapers?

I recall discovering that I would not find the answers from those around me. I would need to get away before I could do anything to change what was taking place. So, for a while, I disappeared, but I kept a votive candle lit in my heart for what I would try to make right some day.

I became active in school, joining chorus, doing variety shows and school plays. I wanted to be an actress because for a while I could become someone else, use someone else's words, emotions, behavior. I could be a bride, a cowgirl, a vamp and a roaring twenties dancer. I joined a forensics group and won a first place trophy for my original speech on "Imagination" and how it could carry us into the future. I danced, I dated, I sketched and wrote poetry and once in a while the face would have tears and the poem would be sad, but I didn't contemplate the signs. I was still staying on top of all of that turmoil by keeping a smile and reaching for as much life as I could outside of my home.

It wasn't until I married and moved away from my family of origin that the first signs of trouble began to appear. I developed severe migraines and had fainting spells. The doctor attributed this to my being on the pill. But as I look back, it was just a time when the first symptom felt it could emerge. I had felt some depression and fluctuating moods, but not to the degree that I would later experience. I unknowingly applied some of my secondary survival skills during this period of my life. I began to jog and spend more time alone. The exercise helped ward off some of the heaviness I was feeling. The time alone helped me to reflect on my situation and overcome what seemed to be troubling me, but the real causes stayed buried.

Another burial of self: while my husband went to college, I held a full time job kept our apartment and became a Big Sister which gave me my first taste of what mothering would feel like. I befriended a very bright and articulate twelve-year-old girl named Mary. She came from a very poor, single-parent family, and each of her sisters had a different father. It was a family so unlike mine, yet I remember being impressed that poverty did not mean abuse. There was love and kindness expressed within this odd family. I remember when Mary found a shriveled-up Christmas tree in a dump-site and brought it home and decorated it. I was in awe of how beautiful she saw this tree that had mostly bare branches and was a reject from the lot. She saw beauty in the tree. I saw beauty in Mary.

It wasn't until the next year of my marriage that a major piece of my childhood unfolded. The first symptom of my sexual abuse occurred in a public restroom. I was sure that my vagina was on fire it was burning so badly. But again, buried the cause, feeling unable to deal with the submerged memory.

Throughout this period and beyond, there were some unsuccessful attempts at burying my pain through alcohol which led to episodes of inebriation and attempted suicide. When I drank, rather than forget the demons of the past, they would surface and torment me. I found myself in the lap of one of the vice-presidents of the company I had been working for, telling him through tears and drink that I had been an abused child. And then I disappeared. I awoke in the emergency room of a local hospital screaming. I had to learn the relationship between alcohol and my deep sense of despair. I found that while I didn't have to stop drinking entirely, the time to cut back from alcohol was during my depressions, because any attempt to control my emotions and behavior during a depression was lost if I added too much alcohol. However, at times, small amounts did relax me. I had to learn where the turning point was between relaxing, and becoming lost.

Thwarting the pain was necessary to survive. I used short term emergency tactics. At times, it was difficult to control my thoughts and I began to obsess to the point where I became exhausted and ill. At this point, the most immediate relief for me was to take a nap and turn off the "tapes" inside my mind. This is a very effective tool even now. Though it lasts only a few hours, it can help me successfully parry a major destructive thought pattern, even a suicidal one. I cannot speak highly enough for naps. They have saved my life at times and have helped me as a parent to refuel when there was a chance that I might lose it with my own children.

Shutting off or blocking out feelings was an important survival technique, so too was protecting myself from being overwhelmed through avoidance. When I was experiencing my memories, either actively in my mind or under the surface, I was acutely aware that the tiniest little pain could make me react like I was being burnt alive or scalded with white hot acid. It could be as simple as bumping myself and I would either cry or scream depending on which emotion was being triggered by my inner thoughts. If I was in a sad mood, a small hurt would make me cry uncontrollably. If I was angry, I might throw something or break glass just to hear the sounds of it smashing on a hard surface, and to watch the splinters explode and scatter. When I was feeling rage, I would let out such blood-curdling screams that at times I was terrified of the sound of the agony in my heart. I was amazed at the volume of emotion that I carried. Much of this drama was played out in private behind locked doors or when I was alone. There were times that I didn't understand what was happening to me. But I couldn't seem to stop the power that was flowing through me. I was outraged! Why was I getting hurt when I was already carrying so much pain? I began to avoid things that gave pain. Though this drama was expressed within my internal self, I wondered what kind of face I was presenting to the outside world. I look back on old photographs of myself and can hardly stand to witness the profound look of depression that I see there.

In trying to eliminate as much pain as I could from life, I once made arrangements to be put to sleep for a medical test that was normally done with a local anesthetic. It wasn't just a fear of the pain, it was fear of what the experience might cause me to feel; what might become dislodged and float to the surface that I had buried so long ago. During a rectal exam where a hose had to be inserted into me, I began screaming and crying hysterically in front of a very shocked doctor and nurse. When I confided later that I had been a victim of sexual abuse, they sensitively did the rest of my testing under sedation. This doctor had a lot of compassion for what I had gone through and told me that many women who have been abused have negative reactions to this kind of intimate probing of the body. He suggested that, as a writer, I share with other women a warning that if they are to have any kind of testing involving the more private parts of their bodies, they should alert the medical staff that the tests may cause trauma.

I learned that survivors need to know that while there are techniques to help them, the path for them might be through the abyss of their own experience as it plays out in their life. I don't think it is possible to make the best choices or to have success all of the time. But we need to continually ask ourselves, "How are you feeling? How are you behaving? What is helping you cope? What is pulling you down?"

When I was a preteen, I acted out my sexual abuse on my Barbie and Ken dolls, yet I didn't realize what I was doing until years later. I used dolls to express the language that I couldn't speak. But unlike the relationship between my grandfather and me, Barbie and Ken were equals, romantically involved. Consenting dolls. This small act helped me to accept my sexual feelings.

I didn't always know what was taking me into survival and recovery. I find, however, looking back that there were some unexpected ways that my child spirit flourished. I started to paint more around the age of thirty. I water-colored parts of Psalm 23 using babies and small children and Jesus as their protector. I could then imagine myself in each of these paintings and could live in them when I needed to find a safe place to hide and be little with God as my protector. Sometimes, when dealing with intensely painful memories I would regress to various stages in my past childhood, at times I would become an infant, other times a toddler or a little girl. Several times in the infant stage, I would find myself in bed curled in the fetal position sucking my thumb. I did not judge these moments or feel embarrassed at my regressive behavior for I knew then as well as I know now that it was an important passage to my healing of childhood wounds. There are messages our child wants to give us that only she or he can communicate.

I found a real source of comfort in physical self-love. Sometimes the body pain is so deep and so intense that the comfort must come from places where desecration took place. All of that shame, fear, humiliation and sense of my own evil was massaged into relief, albeit temporary relief, by allowing myself to pleasure the body that was hurt. This practice started in my childhood partly as a reaction to my sexual molestation. Later, as I grew into a teen, it helped me relieve my growing sexual urges. It has helped me in my marriage at times when I am not able to have sex with my husband, or when orgasm is blocked in sex-sharing. It has taught me immeasurably how complex, and intricate, and responsive my body is when sex is something I choose to enjoy, not someone else's choice used against me. I could write pages on these experiences. They have been so freeing for me. It is something we as a culture need to respect and elevate—the right to love ourselves as a basic human need beginning from infancy. I have taught my children that this practice is normal and healthy.

There is a place for objects in the healing of trauma. Many times abuse is complicated by deprivation and neglect. Little things can give you a sense of your own goodness. After one surgery for the treatment of my infertility, my cousin Bonnie bought me some beautiful delicately-sexy underwear as a gift. It did much to bolster my sense of femininity. Ever since that gift of several years ago, I have kept myself well stocked in pretty underwear. Even if I should look despondent on the outside I can feel that underneath I am still attractive. What you do to feel better may at times seem inconsequential, but for me, covering my places of pain with silky satin and lace gives me a little different perspective. It encourages new thoughts and challenges the sense that I felt "ugly," a feeling all too pervasive for people who have been abused, although it actually only describes how we were treated. Sadly though, for many of us, it has become the major force in determining our self concept.

The act of giving yourself presents can be nurturing as well. Frequently I buy fresh flowers to grace my table, counter or desk. Their fragrance, color, and vital life give me a sense of present beauty and future hope. This is especially helpful in the winter when there is a natural privation of flowers. I sometimes visit a horticulture dome, nursery or florist and just spend a little time among all of that scent and brilliance. I have found some of the nicest people work in places like these. The companionship is nice when too much isolation threatens me.

Laughter can be healing. It can break a bad mood and bring cheer to downhearted spirits. My husband used to stand near me when I went to the humor section of a card store and read greeting cards. I would laugh so hard that my eyes would tear. He enjoyed just listening to this sound which was heard all too infrequently in our home during hard times.

Every survivor needs a confidant. It can be anyone. I had a wonderful therapist, but my confidant turned out to be my next door neighbor who is also my best friend. I knew there was something special about her the first time I met her. I had just moved into the neighborhood and within months ended up in the hospital after swallowing a bottle of sleeping pills. One night, I was taking a walk with my husband and we met our new neighbor on the street in front of our house. She knew from my son that I had been in the hospital and she surmised by his explanation that I had attempted suicide. Within moments of our introduction, I was crying in her open arms. We were friends from then on and continue to be each other's best support. It doesn't matter who becomes your confidant. What matters is that you can tell this person anything and they will listen even when they don't understand.

We started writing letters to each other because being busy mothers with small children and hectic schedules, we couldn't always arrange time together. The times we did, the kids would often dominate with their noise and it was difficult to have any significant conversation. So, I now have a box filled with letters from her and another file of letters I wrote to her that I kept copies of. For me as well as for her, this became a very therapeutic tool. I would write how I was doing and she had time to read, think and respond. It turned our communication into something deeper as we affirmed each other's life.

Writing has always been a catharsis for me, but receiving letters from someone who loves you is an experience that everyone should have. Words on paper seem to last and penetrate. People often share from their heart and soul when writing. I have many letters from her telling me how much I mean to her and why I should not die. It is a gift beyond measure to have someone be so frank and caring. She could do something for me that no one in my extended family ever did, tell me not to die, and she was lovingly convincing. Suicidal feelings still assault me from time to time. But someone in this world wants me around. When I don't have the will to live, I think of her words and those of others who have told me, "Please don't die," and I juxtapose the voices, mine and theirs. It helps me to choose life over death at times.

One of the things I find helpful is to write things down in a journal, poem or story. Photographs will also jog memories for me.

In a writer's group someone shared that looking at photographs with a magnifying glass brings out details not immediately perceptible to the eye. I record what I see, feel and remember. I have saved articles of clothing, artwork, toys and books from different stages of my children's lives and put these things in boxes. These are my memory boxes and they will help me recall an experience or even a picture of what my children were like at certain times.

When my thoughts are negative, that is the time I need to avoid making major decisions. My assessment of things is impaired when I'm struggling. I have a stronger need for affirmation, compliments and praise. I need to hear about my value from others. When I experience paranoia, I avoid reading sensational stories in the newspapers or watching disturbing movies. I read more romance novels or soft poetry. In my angry phases, I need more time away from my children so that I don't hurt them. I do more writing at these times. It becomes a necessary exorcism of what is bothering me. My writing teacher suggested that I write angry letters to those who upset me. I don't send them right away, but wait until I feel better. If they are appropriate, then I send them. If they merely vent anger, I don't. One scathing letter was written in the middle of the night. I was so upset I couldn't sleep. I tore it up the next day and saved a relationship by not sending it. I was glad I wrote it. It got the poison out.

I have had a variety of manifestations throughout my life where parts of my self cried out for attention and care. Migraines, memory lapses, disassociation, vaginal and rectal bleeding, all intensities of depression from mild to severe, attempted suicide, daily headaches, inner voices, blanking out, fits of rage, uncontrollable crying, anxiety attacks, nightmares, feeling insane, flashbacks, isolation behavior, out-of-control spending, alcohol abuse, insomnia, oversleeping, paranoia, and many more that would take me another page to list. Symptoms would appear at times when stress from my life would rub up against a past wound. Once while I was writing a poem on child abuse I began to spontaneously bleed from my vagina. I have had this symptom many times and I associate it with my body's more serious grieving. At such times, when I am too deep into the memory to cry, my body does it for me. At one critical time, I was bleeding from my mouth, my nose, my vagina and my rectum. Blood is a sign for me that my being is experiencing overload. When this happens, I calm things down and take care of my self. I may even need to shift my focus in an act of protection until I am stronger. At one point the bleeding got so bad I had to have a D&C to stop it. Sometimes even the body is not able to carry the weight of grief and anguish. I have learned to respect what my body is telling me. I try to alleviate symptoms by paying close attention to those things in life that cause me stress. When I sense the tension is mounting, I find ways to either decrease the situation or salve the damage that has occurred. I have made "survival lists" of what to do in a time of crisis. I am always looking for new ways to help myself through hard times, thus, my list of things to do is open-ended.

I wouldn't be where I am today without therapy. I question whether I would still be alive without therapy. I can not overemphasize the importance of seeking experienced help on the journey to recovery and health. I have been in some kind of therapeutic relationship since my mid-twenties. I see therapy as a lifelong choice if I am to grow and continue to overcome the past to the point where I will have the kind of freedom that was my birthright. I have not been in therapy continuously. However, I have taken breaks from it, sometimes for a period of two years. When I become dysfunctional or am dealing with a crisis, the first thing I do is go back into therapy to have some help dealing with my problems.

I have worked with social workers, psychotherapists, psychologists, therapists and psychiatrists. I have found my most successful relationships with the first three. I have been under psychiatric care for nearly as many years as I have been in therapy. In my experience, only three out of the seven doctors that I have worked with were actually helpful beyond medication. Others for all of their education seemed unable to help a suffering human being. I needed medication to function. However I stayed with a psychiatrist for years whom I strongly disliked. He would insult me at times, but because I was too afraid to change doctors I stayed trapped. When it came time to work through my sexual abuse and he remarked, "So your grandfather diddled in your crotch", I walked out and never came back. When I finally did change doctors, I discovered that there were good psychiatrists, but I had to do some research first. My therapist helped in this. It was a very costly process to seek psychiatric help and many insurance companies only pay part of the bill. I needed to find a doctor I was comfortable with, who was wise, compassionate and knowledgeable, as well experienced with medication. I felt like a guinea pig when trying to find a medication that would alleviate some of my symptoms. One doctor prescribed an antidepressant for me and said, "See you in two weeks." I had severe side affects. I cut myself, burned myself and hit a car. My thoughts were backwards, I started getting daily headaches and began to accelerate to the point where I couldn't sleep. This doctor was irritated when I called him and interrupted his time at home because I was frightened of what was happening to me. I now have a woman psychiatrist who embodies the things that are important to me. We work as a team on my recovery. It is a joint effort and she respects my insight and wisdom as much as I do hers.

I do not give all of the credit to the therapists, though. Much of the work—actually most of the work—was done by me, the client. The therapist is like a wise god or goddess overseeing the process, making constructive suggestions and lending support when it's needed. What I accomplished was up to me. It was essential first of all that we like each other and could establish a companionable rapport. I have grown to love nearly all of my long-term therapists. And I have felt loved by them. For me, therapy was the first experience of non-violent, non-abusive love.

More recently, separation from my family of origin was a necessary step in my recovery process. This occurred after a family confrontation in 1992 which for me was dissatisfying. I received some hate letters from my father following this family meeting and annihilation from some of my siblings. I had turned forty and it shocked me that I had lived for so many years with these wounds, and that my family still had power to cause more pain and agony for me. I decided to stop communicating and began the process of claiming the woman within. I needed to stop trying to be acceptable to my family. I wanted to feel that they loved me and cared what had happened to me. But during a period of chronic illness that year, I received very little concern from them, and something hopeful in me began to die. I realized that I might never get the nurture from my family that would make me feel whole, and that in order to heal myself, I needed to form a new family from people around me who really did love and care about me. But I also knew that this could not be accomplished right away. It takes months, perhaps years to build a new family. But as I began to fill my life with people who affirmed my existence, I saw more positive effects than I had in decades of trying to draw water from a birth well that could not or would not give sustenance. Separation has been very beneficial to me, although it was one of the most painful choices that I have ever made. In fact, I didn't think I'd live through the agony of those first few months. Coming from a large family affected so many relationships that while breaking away accelerated my growth, the losses have been deep and oppressive. I don't think I have completely recovered from this major step in my life. I am now, however, at the point where I have resumed limited connection with my extended family, and am at peace with this, although the last time I was home, which was for my grandmother's funeral, my sister-in-law told me that she didn't know why my husband hadn't dumped me years ago. How can one fathom being treated like this by people who call themselves "family"? When we celebrated Christmas this past year "with the family," my own relatives were not invited.

Sometimes I questioned why I needed to work at recovery rather than keep things buried. The process often felt as horrific as the original abuse. However, it not only helped me heal, it saved my children from unnecessary pain and will spare their children as well. In a sense, I am changing the world by my act of recovery, moving it bit by essential bit to a place where peace and creative problem-solving replace violence, aggression and cruelty.

As I have been working on recovery I have seen that not everyone survives. It isn't that they necessarily die either. In our large family of eleven children, some of us have succeeded in stopping the cycle of abuse. Others have not been so successful. I have wondered over the years if my focus on the past was necessary or whether I should just forget it and go on with my life. But I realize that because of my willingness to admit what happened and to work through the problems my childhood wounds caused in my life, I can offer a different legacy for my children. Sadly, denial is rampant in my family. Several of my brothers and sisters will not even admit they were abused, and their denial has lead to continuing the abuse into the next generation. One brother who is abusive to his children uses religion as his reason for punishment. In denying his own abuse, he is blind to what he is doing with his children. But his rage leaks out. One day he put his fist through a wall. He was ritually abused as a child, and I am convinced that until he can get out from under the yoke of his religion, which gives him permission to continue corporeal punishment, he will not seek the help he needs for himself, his wife and his children. Yet, he is a loving father. I call this experience of love schizophrenic. Children need love to survive, but in homes where there is violence, getting essential needs met may mean tremendous risk. Not only does the person who inflicts the pain seem like two different people or more, but the child victims split their own personalities so as to receive what they need, while burying the hurt in another part of themselves.

Denial is dangerous. I remember sitting in a little coffee shop until nearly two in the morning crying with one of my sisters who was abusing her small children, yet denying that what she was doing was "abuse." Another sister was with us and the two of us tried to reach out and help this mother in distress. As the years went by, I gave her bits of advice such as, "When rage is upon you, lock yourself in your room away from the kids and take a tennis racket and hit the bed until the anger is spent." She too is a very religious person. More times than I care to number, I have seen how certain religions perpetrate abuse and support abusive parents. Children are beaten to drive the evil from them, but sometimes this strategy backfires. When my sister's son turned fourteen, he beat her up, and put her in the hospital.

There is not nearly enough written or even understood about the effects of verbal abuse on the child. One author calls it the, "murder of the soul." If I had to choose which of my injustices, physical, sexual or verbal was most damaging to me, I might say the verbal abuse caused the most profound emotional scars. It's not something that you can really measure, but the wounds are imbedded deep in your personality. Even today I can hear some of the most vile of statements in my head and I know the voice comes from my mother. When I get angry at myself for doing something wrong or inappropriate or even when I make a mistake, I berate myself so brutally that it will often trigger deep-seated self-hatred and self-destructive tendencies. I have buried these heinous emotions deeply so as to not hurt my children or others whom I love and are close to, but when I have done something I feel badly about, they shoot to the surface.

As children, besides being disciplined too harshly, our spirits were stabbed with insulting words. There are words and expressions that make me flinch: "selfish, lazy, stupid, shut-up, liar, thief, sinner." There are phases that still haunt me. "I will slap you silly." "You lazy good for nothing kid." "Wait until your father gets home." "I'll beat the living daylights out of you," and "I'll give you something to cry about." These are just a few of the things my mother would say and coupled with the look of anger and hate, they permeated my soul with such a feeling of my repulsiveness that I became totally convinced I was evil.

As a result, I couldn't look in the mirror for years without wincing. I hated what I saw. I was frightened of my own face, which would at times contort and form an image of a devil or demon before my eyes. I knew my soul had to be black and that I was and would always be damned. Aggravating my abuse were the obtuse values taught in our family. Our poverty was perceived as a source of shame within the family. It created a feeling of personal poverty: we were poor, thus we were inferior; we lacked value. Adults ruled. Anyone outside of our religion was going to hell. Feelings were ridiculed. Opinions were not allowed if they did not agree with what my parents thought. Challenge to authority was met with violence and rules were reinforced with some form of punishment. Even to laugh at a time when my father was in a bad mood at the dinner table meant being yanked off your chair, kicked or slammed into a wall. The numbing daze that settles over a child's spirit can linger for years, long after the anger is forgotten and the actions retreat behind a veil.

Overcoming and healing from emotional abuse adds to my own sense of goodness and my ability to share this goodness with others. With each new level of health, I get a little more stamina to continue the hard work of recovery. Each success is an offering I can give to my children. Their birthright. It will cost me. But it is a price I gladly pay.

As a mother of two very active children, with a husband and a home to manage, there have been times when I could not keep up with my responsibilities. It is at these times that I lower my expectations and get temporary help. I have used many aides to get me through low times. I bring my husband's shirts to the laundry, I hire someone to clean my house, I employ a baby-sitter to take care of my children or use drop-in centers, I pay a school-aged girl to do my ironing and I tell everyone significantly close to me what condition I am in. We eat more carry-out meals. My husband has had to take time off of work. My neighbors have taken my kids or made a meal for us and occasionally, someone gives me a bouquet of flowers to show they want me to feel better. I schedule more appointments with my therapist. I cancel all appointments that would be too stressful to make. I cut back on time with friends.

There were months where I was bedridden with chronic fatigue and my children would come and lie on the bed to spend time with me. One of the most soul-filling times for me is when I begin to recover, regain my stamina and pick up my life again. I celebrate each thing that I take back as a symbol of my growing health.

Some things of course cost money. But there are ways to get affordable help. Teenagers have been great at doing whatever I needed for a few dollars. They did laundry, played with my children, did yard work or shoveled snow, ran errands, made simple meals, etc. I have also reached out to caring people in my neighborhood to help through hard days and paid back the favor when I was able. I asked at a near-by church if there was an older woman who would like to be grandmother to my little girl when she was a baby. I was going through a suicidal time. The woman who came forward happened to be the wife of a man who worked with my husband. For a year she took my daughter one day a week. We became close friends as well.

I began to relive my childhood experience of sexual abuse in the mid-eighties. It was then that I decided to just record what was coming out. Much of what surfaced from within was told to me in the voice of a battered frightened child. While recalling my sexual abuse, I reached a point where sex with my husband felt like rape. The feelings of the past were so present that I could feel all of the pain, shame, humiliation and fear that I had experienced as a child. At times I was this little child being molested by my grandfather. If my husband and I made love, it traumatized me. I would cry softly in the dark, so quietly that even my husband didn't realize how sex was affecting me. I tried to hide what I was going through. I tried to handle it alone. But things got worse and I went from crying softly to internal screaming and the pain became overwhelming. Finally I had to tell my husband what was happening. I asked him not to make love to me for awhile. He tried very hard to be understanding and though he didn't want to, we became celibate lovers for a year.

At this point I didn't know if I would ever want to have sex again. I didn't know that our celibacy would last only a year. My husband tried so many agonizing times to convince me to try sex, but I kept assuring him that I just couldn't and our marriage would be full without it. I was wrong on this point, but I didn't realize this until years later. A woman I met recently confided that she has been celibate in her marriage for ten years. Though during that year I needed to have the freedom to choose celibacy, I don't believe that long-term celibacy is a healthy choice for a marriage. My husband and I turned to ourselves to fulfill sexual desire and self-love helped, but it does not completely alleviate the necessity for sexual intimacy for a couple. I was prepared to share my husband with another woman if I couldn't be sexual for him, but it never

came to this. Though I felt this might happen, I think it would have added even more complications to an already volatile situation. Celibacy offered me a safety zone from being touched in a way that felt almost worse than the original abuse. I attribute this to my long years of repressing the experience and its effects on me. At times I would leave my body or disappear and the part that held the intensely painful memories was put
to sleep. It may have also been the time when I formed an "alter" self to manifest the experience and bury it within. She, this little blonde child, still hides things that I can't bare to look at.

For Christmas a year ago, my husband bought me one of my most treasured gifts, my first vibrator. It has given me hours of bliss. This year, he bought me another one. I had burnt out the motor on the old one. This new vibrator sends me to the stars. I not only love the present, I love my husband for wanting my pleasure as well as his own. We continue to be more liberated in our sexual play. Getting to that point, however, was a long, arduous journey. But recovery is possible. Just because we are sexually dysfunctional at some point in our lives, does not mean we will remain that way forever. It feels as though it will at the time, but believe me, it can change and you can not only become functional, you can become vibrant and liberated.

I wish that I could say that once I worked through the sexual abuse, I became a free woman. I do believe that this is possible, but I still have to deal with remnants of the past. I still have very sensitive areas of touch even with my husband of twenty years. There are places on my body that I do not want him to touch and he respects this. At times he tests the waters, but I am now able to move his hand if it feels like an invasion. An example of this is that my husband may use his tongue between my thighs but not his fingers. I know why I hate this touch. Years of therapy has not changed this. However, I am free to touch as much as I like because my own feminine fingers do not pose a threat to me. I have control. Another problem area for me is my breasts. I will allow my husband to touch them at times, but this can turn in a matter of seconds to a situation of terror for me. I begin to panic and if I do not stop him, I will start screaming internally. Despite these limitations, we can still enjoy sex. Survivors need to set ground rules and partners of survivors need to respect the untouchable places and focus on those where touch is welcome and desired. It may not make sense to one's partner why touch in a certain place at a certain time might be intolerable, but whether he understands or not or not, we need to protect ourselves from being traumatized in the present. I have tried to be creative with this problem. One night when we were at a hotel and he wanted to fondle me, I felt an immediate repulsion. So as not to ruin the mood, I took the satin belt off of my robe and playfully tied his hands to the bedpost. I then had ultimate control of the sexual activity and he had only to lie back and enjoy the game.

I see my work in recovery as existing beyond myself. I see the need to continue to educate and inform others so that the wounds of the past will be healed to the point where others, too, can eliminate what causes the personality to suffer, repress and split. I know that I have integrated a great deal over the years through therapy. I have a knowledge now that I didn't possess in the past. I am piecing together a lost self and discovering that there is more to me than I ever imagined, and that the basic belief that I grew up with about my self being evil and deserving abuse was a lie.

WHAT ARE YOU WAITING FOR . . .
(an exercise in truth)

if you see it - enjoy it
if you need it - get it
if you're hungry - eat
if you're tired - sleep
if you're hurt - cry
if you're terminal - die
if you love - give
if you live - rejoice
if you're sad - talk
if you're a miracle - walk
if you're old - smile
if you're wrinkled - smile
if you're broken - mend
if you're breathing - bend
if you're lonely - fly
if you're empty - try
if you forgot - learn
if you're trapped - turn

▣ Maria Theresa Maggi

AS THE FRUIT PULLS AWAY

1

You are beautiful and I love you,
but no scent can penetrate
this thick wall of punishment.
Only a sacrifice unfastens what is captive.
Chestnuts marked with crosses open in the fire,
the edges curl back and lick the air.
It is nearly time. In the firelight,
as you dance, your shadow expands
and contracts gracefully on the wall.
Soon, very soon,
I will join you in body
as well as spirit.

2

Breaking down a wall is hard work.
Stepping through the debris,
damp with a layer of sweat and coated
completely with the fine gray dust of broken stone,
I give myself to what I see:
a kitchen filled with sun,
one shiny white plate resting
on a table cleaned of everything
but a paring knife, one peach,
and yellow daisies stuffed in glass.
Tiny, clear pearls of oxygen collect under water,
stud the thick green fuzz of each corrugated stem.
You wait for me at the table, freshly showered,
smelling of clean skin and water, your hair
still wet but combed into place.
We don't speak. Instead,
you slice the peach carefully,
and we listen as the fruit pulls
away from the stone for the last time.

Amanda Powell

EVENING

My mother reads to her mother.
Steady, she does not look up from the page,
their two white heads bent together
undisturbed, crossed oddly by the panes

 of the propped-open window over my grandmother's chair.
 The evening is as peaceful as that prayer,

the one when the heart stops its striving.
From where I stand, the stove-top in the larger window floats
crazily upward out of Chagall. I am giving
the stocks and daisies and roses a good long soak

 up the back hill. At this hour, daylight held in them glows
 a long time in the dusk. No one of us knows—

though here we are now—how we got here from there.

Joan Dobbie

MY EXPERIENCE OF YOGA AS HEALING

I've always been tense. At least since I was two & first came to America. Could be I was born that way, could be I was hurt by my parents' hurts (they were holocaust survivors). Could be a lot of things that no therapist I've ever worked with has been able to figure out. It's a fact of my life that I've lived with. Rarely in my childhood pictures am I smiling. Could I have been abused at some point in my early childhood? Not that I remember. In any case, my early life has been marked by a series of intense traumas broken by periods of being normal, but tense and hurting.

When my first child was born, I fought the delivery body & soul (thought I was coming apart, did not want to give up the pregnancy, thought I would die) & then had a post-partum "psychosis" that died down into a depression which kept me in treatment for over two years, ending completely only 4 years later, when my husband & I separated, and I, 4 months pregnant, went home to my family.

I signed up for my first yoga class after the birth of my second child (who has just turned 20 this week) because someone, it may have been my sister, told me that what I'd learned in Lamaze childbirth training classes was "just a little taste of yoga." The first thing that happened when I started practicing yoga was that I stopped yelling at my children, at least most of the time. The next thing that happened was that I lost interest in smoking. I also stopped eating meat, or even wanting to.

For the first year or so of my practice, old emotions would surface in an almost unbearable way. I would have tears pouring down my face as I performed my sun salutes (a series of 12 postures done in one flowing motion that serves as a warm-up). Waves of anger would roar through me in the midst of a session, and if I was interrupted, heaven help the interrupter! Sometimes there would be too much pain, or else I'd begin to feel unbearably bored, and I'd just quit. But by the end (if I stuck it through) I found I was calm, vibrant, and happy. In time the yoga sessions stopped feeling like a chore and became a great pleasure. I would experience immense joy—even during the session.

My first yoga teacher insisted that we practice for at least 45 minutes a day, & I did that, religiously. Maybe that's why the yoga had such profound effects so quickly. Now, after 20 years of daily practice & 12 years of teaching yoga I can say absolutely that yoga asks nothing of you, except that you do it. Not once. Not twice. But regularly. And it gives in return, if not certain enlightenment, at least a great deal of healing. After a few months of practice, I, who had not written a poem for many years, suddenly found myself full of poetry, writing every spare moment. I started drawing too. Took up photography. All sorts of art found its way into my life. My very vision had changed. Even colors were brighter. My entire experience of life was more vivid.

I would be lying if I said that everything has been marvelous ever since, or that I have never again fallen into the kind of depression or anxiety I seem to have a biological tendency toward. But I will say that as long as I remain regular in my yoga practice I do not lie to myself. I may not like what I'm feeling, but I *know* what I'm feeling. And even when I'm not happy, I'm never a physical or psychological danger to the children in my life.

YOGA CLASS: THE TEACHER SPEAKS

We sit straight
Hold our hands open as cups
Breath deep swelling breaths
My lips form familiar words
But I am not speaking
It is the mother who is speaking
Out through the channel
Of my throat
I am riding on the dark resonance
Of her voice
That is not my voice
But hers
I listen as she speaks
She is telling us now
To come touch each other
I feel other hands move warm into mine
I glance at the clock
We have one human hour
The room is darkening
The mother is saying to close our eyes
We do

And we see vast distances inside of ourselves
We see infinite darkness & there we find color
We are watching our blood flow
In rich salty rivers
We are touching the ivory metal of bones
Our bodies are flowing in rhythm
With the centuries
Slow as a tide moving over an island
We are mists bringing life to dark clay
Making flesh
Moving our flesh over ivory bones
I listen with heart expanding
I listen with mind carefully tuned
I speak but the voice is not mine
All ears are turned inward
The mother is speaking —
Of peace
Her voice that is sweet like the worlds
That are breathing within us
Is speaking of peace
    Is speaking of peace
We are joined in the flow of the breath
Of her breathing
The mother is flowering
    The mother is flowering
I listen I hear words
I listen I hear words & winds
I listen I hear winds & waters
We are swimming in the dark honey
Of the song of our mother
We are holding together like the cells
That make up a creature
We are breathing one breath like the breath
Of the planet
Not sleeping nor waking
And still we are watching
With visions that rise to a place
Some call heaven
We are joined in a blessing
That is ours for the asking
We are vessels of peace
    We are vessels of peace

Quinton Hallett

SHOOTING STARS

We lie parallel
on our backs outdoors,
darkness and red wine separating us
across the deck.
"There's one!" you cry.
I don't see it.
Then you miss the first bat,
lit from below by our candle,
shooting through the dusk,
so we're even.

It's never bothered us,
seeing constellations emerge
at different rates, that eyesight
and what we remember of astronomy
are not exactly alike.
But we've been at this long enough
to know that every now and then
we must tilt our faces in the same direction.

Kim Holloway

FRACTAL

The word, "fractal," came up at the beach yesterday. "A portion of a dimension," my friend Star said, "We've all heard of one-dimensional, two-dimensional, three-dimensional, even enjoyed the music of the Fifth Dimension (once upon a time), or shuddered at aliens from the fourth dimension in some science fiction story. But a fractal is a piece of a dimension."

We were sitting on the beach, enjoying that plush October weather, with its golden light and warm haze. This particular beach is the town's old dump. Decades of bottles, crockery, and plates have smashed and washed against the rocks until the beach sings with the music of polished glass as this giant lapidary smoothes the edges of depression glass, milk glass, cut glass, beer glass, pale yellow tiles, hand-painted platters, ceramic pipes. You're lucky to find a fragment as big as your palm. For Tommy, my foster son, it was a giant treasure chest; he chirped and shrieked with delight and immediately loaded his patch pockets with so many "jewels" that he had to hold on to his waistband to keep from having his pants around his knees. Finally, he found an old sock, filled it to the brim with smooth colored treasures, then sat for a long time watching tiny crabs sidle in and out of the rocks.

I don't know if what Star said is true, but if so, "fractal" is a word I've been looking for. Tommy's past is a fractal.

It's exactly a year since we had the call from Child Protective Services. It was three o'clock on a Monday afternoon; the social worker began with, "Can you come pick him up tomorrow at noon?"

"Him—who?" I blurted. We'd been a licensed foster-adoption home for more than a year without a single call. We'd read everything from Bettelheim to Spock, taken a year of foster- parenting classes with Social Services, changed our work schedules, "child-proofed" our home, and examined our lives, motives, strengths and weaknesses until there was nothing left to do but realize we were as ready as we were going to get.

A string of questions caught in my throat. "What's his name? How old is he? What language does he speak? What color is he?"

"He" turned out to be a four-and-a-half year old emergency placement by Child Protective Services for abuse and neglect.

Our first week together went according to the foster care textbooks. Tommy, a frightened, quiet boy on his best behavior had come to live with us. After a week, it was apparently safe enough for cracks in his composure to show. When he spilled a glass of milk, he hid, curled into fetal position, under the dining room table, terrified. "What will you do?" he whispered. It took an hour to coax him out. And we soon learned there's no such thing as childproofing; all the gadgets in the world merely give you a little more time to avert disaster. And try child- proofing anything when you don't know whether the child will be 10 months or 6 years old!

We also learned that all the textbook preparation in the world is still only ink on paper—theory. In practice, finding the appropriate response to a child who says, "Why did you look over there?" when caught sneaking, stealing or lying, a response that won't push him further into deception and dissimulation, is tough. Finally, with the help of a fine therapist (with separate sessions for the boy and for us), I've learned to come up with comments like, "Well, that didn't turn out like you thought it would, did it?" on my own.

But those first few weeks of our relationship gave us little time for reflection. We got to know Tommy via total immersion in the moment. My partner and I did our best to pay attention, to stay present, to cope; understanding would have to come later.

He ate anything and everything we put in front of him, astonishing my partner and me one night by eating 5 chicken tacos without a pause. He hid peanut-butter-and-jelly sandwiches under his mattress, crackers and cheese in his drawers and pockets, and was frantic that there might not be enough food.

He hated naps, hated sleep, and was terrified of the dark. Every night the sheets were soaked. We bought a plastic sheet and washed the blankets and linens every day. He said, "I like to pee in the bed, then it's warm and cozy." That was his longest sentence. When he fell down and skinned both knees, he refused to cry, or even take a deep breath, his little body absolutely rigid. Water is the one thing we found that soothes him, whether it's paddling in the tub or shower, helping wash the dishes, or splashing after the goldfish in our little pond.

Less than a month after he came to live with us, I went in to wake him from a long, unusual nap. He was deeply asleep, in fetal position, his small sweaty fists clenched tight, contortions of anguish, fear and rage passing quickly over his face. As he slowly awoke, he became more and more upset. The bed was soaked, and he began to cry out, "No, no, no!" I carried him out to the front room and sat on the couch, with him in my lap. Every time he began to open his eyes, the "no's" would become louder. He struggled not to cry. I told him it was okay. Okay to cry, okay to be angry, okay to feel whatever he felt. After several minutes of resistance, he "let go" and went deep into a powerful, forty-minute-long sobbing and shrieking episode, repeating, "I wanna go home," over and over again. Once he whimpered, "I miss my friend Jacob." And twice he said, "I want my mom." His sobs stopped only when he was completely exhausted. My arms ached and trembled from holding him so that he wouldn't bang his head on the furniture or the floor. He never struck out in anger to hurt me or himself, he just had so much locked inside, so much anger, so much fear.

I could go on forever. But I cannot let you in to this child's life in a sentence, or a page, or perhaps even a book. It would take another lifetime to fill you in. And I can only offer fractals, portions of a dimension not my own. Not a crisp, clean fraction or even a fragment—a fractal.

I could tell you then and now stories: It has taken us a year to piece together his medical records, to know in my bones what he looks like from across the playground. The latter seems such a simple thing, and is probably instinctive for birth parents. But for weeks I was terrified I'd focus on the wrong child at a distance of fifty yards if I didn't memorize what he was wearing.

When he came to live with us, he couldn't count past "one." Didn't know the alphabet song. Now we're working our way to one hundred, and practice singing the alphabet backwards. His first night with us, he called from the bathtub, "Send in the girl!" Three months later he called me, "that woman who belongs to me." Now he describes me as his mom to other children and adults, but calls me directly by my first name. I could tell you that a year after his arrival, we're still dealing with nightmares, though they've gone from more than a dozen in one night to only several a week. He sleeps with one light on now instead of the whole house blazing. But that information is cold, misleading. As if healing is evinced by book learning or quiet sleep. As if by knowing fragments of history—his story—we might understand how he thinks, how he might respond, what he broods about on a quiet beach. At four and a half he was an expert on sex, drugs and violence. Where will he be at 40, I wonder. All I can tell you is that I want to be there.

Home language skills have changed from, "That be idea!" to, "Well, I hit that boy that because God made me, and God let me do that!" His public school language in extremis remains on the level of, "You fucking bitch!" He can peg the emotional weaknesses of a teacher's aide in less than 30 minutes. The unaware have been reduced to tears in moments. He's been kicked out of every play group and day care in the area. I admire his courage, am saddened and enraged that his hard-won survival skills are now worthless, and deal with the fallout.

"A child's life is simple," my aunt used to tell me. "You've got nothing to worry about, everything is taken care of for you." And what about my foster son's world, where nothing has been taken care of, where everything is to worry about? He lives in a world where the smallest discipline can precipitate, "Do you hate me? I hate myself!" He is astonished that we don't spank. This beautiful boy believes that all grownups are mean to children in the same way that he knows he has two feet.

My partner and I try to teach him new life skills—ones that will last. Ones that will keep his heart open to love, to risk, to possibility. This morning he told me he loved me. Every day is different. Every day is new.

Dorianne Laux

THE TOOTH FAIRY

They brushed a quarter with glue
and glitter, slipped in on bare
feet, and without waking me
painted rows of delicate gold
footprints on my sheets with a love
so quiet, I still can't hear it.

My mother must have been
a beauty then, sitting
at the kitchen table with him,
a warm breeze lifting her
embroidered curtains, waiting
for me to fall asleep.

It's harder to believe
the years that followed, the palms
curled into fists, a floor
of broken dishes, her chainsmoking
through long silences, him
punching holes in his walls.

I can still remember her print
dresses, his checkered Taxi, the day
I found her in the closet
with a paring knife, the night
he kicked my sister in the ribs.

He lives in Oregon now, dying
slowly of a rare bone disease.
His face stippled gray, his ankles
clotted beneath wool socks.

She's a nurse on the graveyard shift.
Comes home mornings and calls me.
Drinks her dark beer and goes to bed.

And I still wonder how they did it,
slipped that quarter under my pillow, made
those perfect footprints . . .

Whenever I visit her, I ask again.
"I don't know," she says, rocking, closing
her eyes. "We were as surprised as you."

Roseann Lloyd

ANGLES OF VISION

for Judith M. Herman, M.D.
Author of *Trauma and Recovery*

In any war story, but especially a true one, it's difficult to separate what happened from what seemed to happen... The angles of vision are skewed. When a booby trap explodes, you close your eyes and duck and float outside yourself... The pictures get jumbled; you tend to miss a lot. And then afterward, when you go to tell about it, there is always that surreal eemingness, which makes the story seem untrue, but which in fact represents the hard and exact truth as it seemed.

—Tim O'Brien
The Things They Carried

when I'm walking
it's the movement
that counts thinking
whatever flits across
the way a cat tracks
each purple shadow
catching the grass
& when I'm walking
I let myself
think about the doctors
who thought my symptoms
indicated a tumor
buried deep
inside my head the
headaches the tunnels
of dazzling light
the weeping
breasts their hands
wrapped my chest
and legs in a blanket
of lead a grasshopper's
thorax I was held down
like when my father
was on top of me & my mind

couldn't skip around
they turned my head
by the chin
like a lover positioned it
so they could see
what was wrong with
their pinpoints
of invisible light
& when I'm walking
I can see the X-rays
they showed me
mainly what you see
is skull
a chalky shadow
something you think
you don't get
until you're dead & bone-
clean   dead & buried
like my brother
who got buried
the year before   his hair
was thick & curly
I never saw his skull
I felt dead then
I couldn't think
about death   couldn't say
the word *incest*
which was buried
with all my feelings
held down by my
thorax
of symptoms
headaches   blinded
vision   weeping
breast milk   no
connection to anything
not even my moon   my
husband's body
heavy & remote
& he strange as my
father   my brother's
gaunt hip-bones

graceful as a girl
walking through
my mind   all the days
I couldn't get up
off the couch

& when I'm walking
I can see the gone
days   those days
on the couch   we lived
in the mountains
then my husband's sunlit
body didn't want any part
of maniacal fathers
dying brothers   not any
part of the truth I could
only see in the screen of
nightmares glimpses
in the morning
light   it was then
I started walking
walking the muddy
back roads across the
floodplain & up through
the fat thistles of the purple
Knappweed & on up
even farther to the canyon
walking up to the
cedars & pines
up to the cold
streams & with each step
the headaches
receded memories
rushing in like the
cold water
like the spring
floods swelling
the valley floor

& when I'm walking I let
myself remember her—
that young woman with

downcast eyes
covered by the long
blond hair   the woman
I used to be—
& I welcome
the remembering
how I made her say the words
out loud in plain
English   without the
benefit of metaphor
my father sexually
assaulted my body
my father beat
down his sons
my youngest brother
refused to fight in Asia
but he died from the
Asian flowers blooming
in his veins—
that's no metaphor   that is
the flower of addiction
what we thought was beauty
was really pain:
don't tell the secrets
death rhymes with incest
—the family twins!
my father is a Gemini—
do you see how fast
my directness can slip away?

& when I'm walking I feel
directly all my
feelings that want to
slip away   the fear &
& sadness & shame & anger
that wanted to hide
my anger at my brother's
death   all mixed up
with Vietnam & the war
& its poppies that
took him anyway & the death
anger   all mixed up

with my body's anger
at my father's military
assaults transferred
from the South Pacific
to the home & to
my grownup home my
husband's violent
silence & when
I'm walking I
welcome the remembering
& I can see
that I don't feel dead
anymore   I can see
I have talked &
raged & cried & stormed
myself back to life
all the way back from
the numbness
from the death thought
that my brother's life = my
life   now I feel
my own blood flowing
through my veins

& when I'm walking
I'm walking life back
into my scared stiff
body that always did
what it was told & when
I'm walking I can
even think about
all the dead weight
that kept me down
the thorax of
symptoms   the doctors'
bewilderment   the rules
& threats in the name of love
black-outs numb hands
nightmares   hands & fists
& silence & fear
of all of the above
& I'm not afraid any more

when I'm walking
I forgive the men the
violence their bodies
have spent on mine—
all their rage & grief—
I let them have
their lives & when I'm walking
I let myself have mine I
let myself think
of my friends & my lover—
the men unafraid to look me
in the face   unafraid
to see the damage
my brothers
I have to keep moving
& there are no more
headaches   even in the city
I'm walking up the canyon
walking with my brother's
lovely hips up through
the Knappweed   up to
the purple Lupine   the Fringed
Gentian the Scarlet Gilia
& on up to the Shooting Stars
walking into my life walking
up the canyon   I never
reach the end

M. Eliza Hamilton

THE PLACE WHERE I AM

The journey
of Fear
and Remembering

ends here

at the center
of the Self
I have uprooted

    to root again

in this space
gutted and razed

once more

there is rain
and air
for roots
to take hold
of me

Me

being born
every minute

every moment
roots delving
deeper

in my Self

the journey
of Fear
and Remembering
    ends here.

Chriss–Spike Quatrone

THE GIFT

I am writing you a poem of my life.
Because you did not run away from my rage.
Because you did not hide from these scars
which I held out to you shyly
for healing.

You held me in circles. In circles,
I dared at first to name the abuse,
to write what I know.
I write what I have known of my life.
And I write my dreams,
urging them into vigorous flight
as I walk.

As I walk beyond
this strange and twisted place,
I remember you a blaze of stars
and a bundle of wind on my back.
In healing and in celebration,
I remember.

Emily Robertson

MIGRATION

Push.
Flower, push
your head through.
The sun is shining
The rain is refreshing
right here on the other side.
Push.
Flower, push
your head through
into strange air
And bloom.

TENDER IS THE FLIGHT

i be light as a single dove feather
    i let the air toss me
turn me
belly-up and belly-down
    i see the world   from a clouds
point of view
y'all look so small down there
when i get
    trapped in the web of a rainfall
i land in grandmas garden
atop a fat gerdenia, fragrant as any
visit home
i inhale the petals breath
and rest and rest
till a southern wind come carry me up
birds of a feather flock together
but i
be light as a single dove feather
i be uplifted on the slightest breeze
i be with the music, like swimmin'
in the sky
hush so i can hear the stars celestial gossip
oh! y'all look so small down there
pity y'all can't see me; pity y'all can't
be me
adrift on my magic carpet breeze

DOGWOOD

Dogwood, white star unfolding spring, beneath you I lay on the ground looking up at the sky through your branches. I was like you, unfolding white petals, star-shaped. Your petals made little skirts. All through the summer you were green and gold, sunlight soaking your leaves. I played in the swamp. My eyes filled with lupines and tiger lilies; my hands were full of stones given by the river, gold and green. There was a place full of salamanders, their orange bodies spotted black like the tiger lilies. Things whose bodies were made of fire and had gold eyes slid through my hands like water.

Lights in the forest at night sat low on the ground and moved away when I chased them. The wind came up at night to my window and woke me. Then we ran downstairs together and out into the moon. The moon full and round called me out to dance. The pines, the moon, the granite, all sang and sang. I made wreathes with my feet and birds with my hands.

The dogwoods's leaves were tinged with red when it began. And then red tears fell, beautiful luminous red leaves against the green-black pines and black sky full of snow. My little child, my beautiful little stone, my piece of clay, my bird. My small thing, your fingers warm and sticky. It is the blackest part, the indistinguishable black and gold and red. The pain that hums out of you, the turning of the earth. My little animal, soft, soft, with very sharp teeth.

This is the beginning of the thread that winds round and round my heart. It cuts and scars. Many years later, I realize that a snake has been living inside of me, a red snake with gold eyes. Snake, coiled up and seething, bites her own tail to keep from shrieking. When I find the snake who lives inside me in such misery, I visit her and give her things to eat. She eats only red things. I feed her and bathe her, lying in a pool of the mother's blood beneath a desert sky under a full moon. She starts to uncoil. It is very painful because she hasn't moved for a long time. She is frightened because of the cord that started to wrap around my heart and choke me, but now that cord has become a very sharp spike that I use to kill my enemies. So she sees that it is safe to come out. She comes bringing beautiful glossy offerings, beautiful scrolls filled with stories, stories of women and people and the world.

The snake is tired and wants to curl up at the base of a tree and sleep beside the river all night. All night, the river rocking her. All night, the river rushing by, singing songs. Meanwhile her sister sleeps inside me, in the round gold room filled with roses. Sleeping, sleeping, my little heart, my petal, my glittering garnet. Maybe you will teach me to pray, teach me to talk, teach me to sing. It is all the same, and I haven't forgotten entirely.

RESOURCE DIRECTORY

The following list of resources is intended to help readers find local professional therapy or support groups. Inclusion in this list does not indicate a recommendation or endorsement by the editor of this anthology. You must use your own judgment in finding the type of intervention that is most helpful to your personal recovery. These organizations represent a cross-range of what is currently available. When writing to any of them, please include a self-addressed stamped envelope to expedite a response.

American Association of Sex Educators, Counselors, and Therapists (AASECT), 435 N. Michigan Avenue, Suite 1717, Chicago, IL 60611-4067, (312) 644-0828. A national certifying organization that can provide you with a list of counselors, psychologists, and other care providers who are certified sex therapists in your area.

American Coalition for Abuse Awareness (ACAA), P.O. Box 27959, Washington, DC 20038-7959, (202) 462-4688. A pro-survivor activist group.

C. Henry Kempe National Center for the Prevention and Treatment of Child Abuse and Neglect, 1205 Oneida Street, Denver, CO 80220, (303) 321-3963.

Childhelp USA, P.O. Box 630, Hollywood, CA 90028. Provides training, consultation, and resources for child abuse victims and adult survivors.

Healing Hearts, c/o Bay Area Women Against Rape (BAWAR), 357 MacArthur Blvd., Oakland, CA 94610, (510) 465-3890. A national organization for ritually abused survivors and their therapists.

The Healing Woman, a monthly newsletter edited by Margot Silk Forrest. P.O. Box 3038, Moss Beach, CA 94038. (415) 728-0339. An excellent resource for anyone in recovery.

Incest Survivors Information Exchange, Box 3399, New Haven, CT 06515. Produces a newsletter for adult survivors.

Incest Survivors Anonymous, Inc., P.O. Box 17245, Long Beach, CA 90807-7245, (310) 428-5599. A self-help peer support group for incest survivors, using a twelve-step model. Will provide you with information on twelve-step groups in your area.

Institute for Transformational Studies, P.O. Box 463, Fond du Lac, WI 54936-0463, (414) 921-6991. Offers a twelve-step support group starter kit, and other resources.

Looking Up, P.O. Box K, Augusta, ME 04332, (207) 626-3402 (fax). Publishes a newsletter and provides referrals, educational presentations, workshops, and wilderness trips for non-offending survivors of child sexual abuse.

MALE (Men Assisting, Leading and Educating), P.O. Box 380181, Denver, CO 80238-1181. An organization for non-offending men survivors of child sexual abuse. Publishes the newsletter, *Men's Issues Forum*, and provides information, workshops, and referral services.

National Child Abuse Hotline: (800) 422-4453.

National Coalition Against Sexual Assault (NCASA), 123 S. Seventh Street, Suite 500, Springfield, IL 62701, (217) 753-4117. Offers referrals for sexual assault victims in Illinois.

National Committee to Prevent Child Abuse, 332 S. Michigan Avenue, Suite 1600, Chicago, IL 60604-4357, (312) 663-3520. Clearinghouse for educational materials on preventing child abuse.

Survivors' Healing Center, P.O. Box 8491, Santa Cruz, CA , (408) 423-7601.

Survivors of Incest Anonymous, (408) 459-8418. Information for help in the Santa Cruz, California area. Offers twelve-step work in many formats. Many communities have such twelve-step groups.

VOICES in Action Inc., P.O. Box 14309, Chicago, IL 60614, (312) 327-1500. A national network for incest survivors and their partners and other support people. Publishes a newsletter, organizes a national conference, and provides referrals.

CONTRIBUTORS' BIOGRAPHICAL NOTES

Jane Bailey is a registered nurse and a student. Her poetry has appeared in *Fireweed* and *Calapooya Collage*. In 1994, she received the Academy of American Poets Prize at Portland State University. Bailey writes, "I am rarely surprised by the extent of domestic violence and its effects, but am often stunned by the strength and resiliency of the human spirit. For a long time I was convinced that the part of me that was murdered by sexual abuse and family violence could never be resurrected. Nature, with its cycles of birth and death and rebirth, has been an invisible seed of hope, repeatedly astonishing me with blossoms that rise where there used to be snow, and fruits that emerge from a once barren winter tree."

Henri Bensussen dedicates the poem, "Chop Chop" "to my mother, who passed on to me the lessons she learned so well from her own mother." "Except at Night / We Dream" is a distillation of the stories told with great emotional pain by women students at an anti-rape speakout held on the Stanford University campus a few years ago.

Laure-Anne Bosselaar grew up in Belgium, and is a graduate of the Warren Wilson M. F. A. Program for Writers. Among other publications, her work has appeared in*The Massachusetts Review*,*The Denver Quarterly, The International Quarterly, The Sycamore Review,* and the *Bellingham Review.* She loves loving life with her husband and children, poetry, music, cooking, speaking Flemish to her plants, and doing it all in Snowmass Village, Colorado.

Donna J. Braswell-Mussato writes that she is "an old poet," born in Oak Park, Illinois, May 19, 1941. She has kept diaries and journals all her life. Now, from her writing room, she looks through oak tree branches, writes poetry, recalls memories of the Southside of Chicago; Dallas, Texas; Cobham, Surrey, England; the Scottish Highlands; the Gap of Dunloe in Ireland where she "would like to spend summers, dance the jig at Mary's cottage, and drink dark beer." In her tree house in Northern California she feels safe and at peace.

Jeanne Bryner is a poet who works as a nurse. She credits her art to the thing that saved her life: her husband's arms. She is a free-lance softball coach, seamstress and mom. Occasionally, she sweeps and dusts.

Melissa Capers writes, "I have written fiction, nonfiction, and poetry, and find that prose is the place I feel most able to articulate my truths. I have become intrigued with how the truth is sometimes best spoken through fiction, sometimes nonfiction. In my life outside writing, after 25 years of living in the south, I am preparing to leave, to discover what I can learn and learn to say outside this environment."

Crystall Carmen was seventeen when she wrote the autobiography that appears in this volume. She is currently making her dream come true by studying Theater Arts in Philadelphia.

Elizabeth Claman's poetry chapbook, *Peripheral Visions*, was published by Five Fingers Press in 1989. The same year, she won the Grand Prize in *Negative Capability*'s Eve of Saint Agnes poetry competition, judged by Diane Wakoski. She has also won two grants from Oregon's Literary Arts, a Pushcart nomination, and a scholarship to Squaw Valley Community of Writers. Her poetry and fiction have appeared in such publications as *Hurricane Alice, River Styx, Mississippi Mud, Two Girls Review,* and *Bastard Review*. Currently, in addition to working on a dissertation for her Ph.D. in Comparative Literature, and compiling anthologies for Queen of Swords, she works as the Fiction Editor for the *Northwest Review*.

Marion Cohen is currently awaiting publication of *Epsilon Country*, her second book of caregiver poems. She has written extensively on this topic, drawing on her own experiences with her husband, who is chronically disabled. In addition to being a writer, she is also a mathematician (Ph.D. from Wesleyan University), and is pleased that she has begun recently to do research again after a long hiatus.

The poems and short stories of **Alice Crane** have been published by *James River Review, Southern Beat,* and other journals. She is a contributing editor of *Southern Beat* and is currently working on a novel.

Peter Cooley is originally from the Midwest, although he's made his home in New Orleans for the past nineteen years. He has published five books of poetry, the most recent being *The Astonished Hours* (Carnegie Mellon, 1972). His work has appeared in *The Atlantic,* the *New Yorker, Poetry, Esquire, The Nation* and other magazines. He teaches Creative Writing at Tulane University. He is married and has three children. At the moment he is working on a new volume of poetry entitled *Sacred Conversations*.

Billie Custock is a professional woman, mother, and grandmother, who, through writing and other art forms, is healing from the aftermath of severe physical and sexual abuse inflicted throughout childhood. In finding her voice, she writes that she is "releasing the numbness, the rage, the pain, and the sorrow" of her past.

Joan Dobbie writes, "My parents were WWII Jewish refugees from Vienna. I was born in Switzerland, but grew up in a small town in northern N.Y. in a home where nearly everything was **not** talked about. I sometimes think of myself as suffering from post-generational traumatic shock disorder. As an adult, a poet, and poetry teacher I stress reaching for truth no matter how uncomfortable. 'Yes, It Is True' is my own truth. 'The Desert & Sea Mother' is drawn from a friend's childhood." Dobbie has a 1988 M.F.A. in Creative Writing from the University of Oregon. Her work has been widely published, mostly in anthologies including *Looking For Home, Women Writing about Exile,* which won a 1990 American Book Award.

Christine E. Donovan is a commercial artist and poet living in Santa Cruz, California. Her poetry often touches on family and social issues. She draws upon her own childhood experiences to enhance her writing.

Sue Doro was a machinist for thirteen years. Her poems and prose have been published in the *Village Voice, Chicago Tribune, Washington Post,* and various women's and labor magazines as well as anthologies such as *Paper Work* (Harbour Publishing 1992), *If I Had A Hammer* (1992), *I Am Becoming The Woman I've Wanted* (1994), both from Papier Mache Press, and *Liberating Memory: Our Work and Our Working Class Consciousness* (Rutgers University Press, 1995). Doro's writing is also taught in Women's Studies courses at Harvard and Rutgers Universities among others, and she is the author of three books of poetry and prose on the subject of her blue collar work experience and its relationship to family and personal life: *Of Birds And Factories* (1982), *Heart Home and Hard Hats* (Midwest Villages and Voices, 1986), and *Blue Collar Goodbyes* (Papier Mache Press, 1993).

Frances Driscoll has had recent poems in *Massachusetts Review, Sojourner*, and *Volt.*

W. D. Ehrhart is the author of seven books of poetry, three nonfiction narratives, and a collection of essays. His most recent book is *The Distance We Travel,* a collection of poems from Adastra press, 1993. He is currently a Pew Fellow in the Arts for Poetry. He has been married for thirteen years and has a seven-year-old daughter.

Susan Eisenberg is a poet/writer, activist, union electrician, installation artist and mother of Zoe and Simon. She has been exploring the spillovers of violence from childhood to adulthood, from the home to the work place. She is author of the poetry collection, *It's a Good Thing I'm not Macho* (Whetstone Press, 1984), as well as a new manuscript, *Knocking at the Windows of My Dreams.* Her work has also appeared in *Sojourner, The Nation, The Seattle Review,* and *Home Planet News.*

Karl Elder's fourth collection of poems is *A Man in Pieces* (Prickly Pear Press, 1994). His previous collections are *Can't Dance an' It's Too Wet to Plow, The Celibate*, and *Phobophobia.* Among his honors are a Lucien Stryk Award for Poetry, and grants from the Illinois Arts Council. He holds the Fessler Professorship in Creative Writing at Lakeland College near Sheboygan, Wisconsin.

K. D. Emerson is a pseudonym for a writer living in West Sacramento, California, with two cats and occasional stray humans.

Suzan Erem is a union activist and communications coordinator for a large union in Chicago. She has been the featured poet at a number of venues in Chicago and has had poems published in two other anthologies—one on substance abuse and another of antiwar poetry. She is the mother of a three-year-old daughter whom she intends to protect as best she can. Her poem, "From Your Daughter, 20 Years Late," was inspired by a newspaper story of two 30-something sisters who discovered their children were being molested by "grampa" who was a university professor. As they explored it further, they realized that they had both also been molested by the man when they were children. When he was thrown in jail, his wife, their mother, bailed him out. Erem writes, "I thought that merited a poem!"

Martin Jude Farawell's chapbook *Genesis: A Sequence of Poems* was published by New Spirit Press in January 1995. His poems have appeared in a variety of journals, including *Amelia, Bitterroot, Hiram Poetry Review*, and *The Southern Review*. He is a graduate of New York University's Creative Writing Program and the recipient of a writing fellowship from the New Jersey State Council on the Arts. Farawell lives in Milford, Pennsylvania with his wife, writer Cheryl Solimini.

Molly Fisk has work forthcoming in *Manoa* and *Harvard Review* and is a four-time nominee for the Pushcart Prize. Her limited edition, hand letterpress volume *Salt Water Poems* (Jungle Garden Press) came out in 1994, as did *Surrender*, a 45 minute spoken word audio tape of her work. Her full-length collection: *A Question About the World* is a finalist for the 1995 Walt Whitman Award and the University of Arkansas Poetry Prize. Fisk is the recipient of a 1995 Marin Arts Council Individual Artist's Grant, and serves as the poetry editor for the West Marin quarterly *Estero*. She is a contributing editor for *The Healing Woman* and teaches with California Poets in the Schools.

Renée Freiheit (a pseudonym) is a young packrat who lives near the ocean, laughs a lot, and owes just about everything that matters to her dear friends.

Barrie Gellis believes "America suffers from an epidemic of child abuse (sexual, physical, psychological, and neglect) which continued after Freud missed the point on incest." He lives in Flushing, New York with his wife, who is an incest survivor. Together they have two shows on cable TV, *The Naked Truth*, and *UFOs Today*. Gellis feels the solution to the unaddressed problem of incest and other forms of abuse is to "treat abused kids today before they become the killers, rapists, and abusers of tomorrow."

Lynn Gerber is a wife, mother of two boys, and a former apparel and textile designer. Presently, she is an administrative assistant and poet—who barely wrote a postcard till six years ago when memory exploded, blew the lid off repression, and pushed feelings through ink. She makes up for lost time by writing and writing. Some of her poetry is published in *Mediphors, Atom Mind, Black Bough Haiku* and *National Library Of Poetry*, and is forthcoming in *Pleiades*, and *Feelings*. She has been a featured reader at cafés and libraries throughout NYC and on Manhattan Cable TV.

John Gilgun earned an M.F.A. and Ph.D. from the University of Iowa. He has won a number of awards for his collections, *Everything that Has Been Shall be Again* (Bieler Press, 1981), and *The Dooley Poems* (Robin Price, 1991). His other books are *Music I Never Dreamed Of* (Amethyst, 1989), nominated for the Lamda Literary Award for "the best gay novel of 1990," and *From the Inside Out* (Three Phase, 1991). Of *The Dooley Poems* Sam Hamill wrote, "Gilgun gets beyond the surface into spirituality ... his poems—and this book—delight." Currently, Gilgun teaches at Missouri Western State College.

Patricia Rose Gilles is a freelance writer, poet and artist, living in Plymouth, Minnesota. She has two children, a son who is twelve, and a daughter, five. Of her work she writes, "The best legacy we can give the next generation is our commitment to exposing and obliterating violence in the home, a breeding ground for violence in our world."

Tamarah Petty Ha is a 29 year-old Amerasian adopted from Seoul, Korea in 1971. She has finally succeeded in leaving an abusive marriage after five years of hell, and is on the long, slow road to recovery. Her poem in this volume, like her other writing, is part of that process. She writes, "Some say adopted children are extra special, because we were actually chosen to be someone's child. But what if those doing the choosing are not meant to be parents?"

Quinton Hallett is a former art administrator who turned to writing full-time at 39. She has published, read and continues to write poetry, short fiction and essays which probe the jagged edges—good and bad—of family and other relationships. She has won awards in Oregon and Arkansas for poetry and fiction. Her poetry chapbook, *Quarry* was published by When the Sun Tries Books Press in Austin, Texas. She is married to artist Dennis Gould and lives with him, two cats and the denizens of 15 rural acres in Noti, Oregon.

M. Eliza Hamilton is 29 years old. She writes, "As a child, writing was the only voice I had and the only way to keep sane amidst the violence done to me within and outside of my home. We must continue to witness to each other's pain and each other's healing. We must remember that we are not alone in this walk. Women have the ancient knowledge and power to heal themselves and each other. Those of us who remember the rites must teach those who do not. No one will do it for us but us."

Mary Diane Hausman writes, "Growing up in Texas has provided me with a particular flavor to add to my writing. I use the images and memories of that place as backdrop to my stories. 'Discoveries' is part of a novel about growing up in Texas. Cassie Mae's life is based on my own, but I don't want her to be a victim, any more than I want to be a victim. Rather, I want the stories to provide a way out of the pain of those hard memories, while at the same time reflecting the strength, compassion and a power to take control, that has also come from those experiences." Hausman's work has appeared in *At The Crossroads, Color Wheel, Relevant Times, Women and Recovery* and *Art: Mag*, as well as other anthologies. She was awarded first place in the 1994 Pennwriters In Other Words Contest for her essay, "The Feeding." She now lives in New Jersey where she writes and teaches workshops on using writing as a healing tool.

Barbara Hendryson is a native San Franciscan. She was educated at City College in San Francisco, the College of Notre Dame in Belmont, and did graduate work in Creative Writing with William Dickey at San Francisco State University. Most recently, her poems have appeared in *The Berkeley Poetry Review, Calyx, Hurricane Alice,* the *San Francisco Bay Guardian, Sequoia, Visions International,* the *Wisconsin Review* and the 1992 anthology, *Cries of the Spirit*. Her work is also included in the forthcoming anthology from Mariposa, *Unheard Voices—Sixteen Poets: Survivors of Incest and Sexual Abuse.*

Donna Hilbert's short story collection, *Women Who Make Money and the Men Who Love Them,* was published in England in July 1994 as a Staple first edition. Her books of poetry are *Deep Red,* 1993; *Mansions,* 1990, both from Event Horizon Press. Her novella, *Waiting for my Baby,* is forthcoming, also from Event Horizon. She lives in Cerritos, California.

Richard Hine was born in London in 1963 and now lives in New York City. His fiction has appeared in *Dexter Review, London Magazine, Loyalhanna Review* (where "Robert's Affair" first appeared), *Treasure House, Whiskey Island Magazine* and other publications.

Kim Holloway is the pseudonym of a Northern California poet and singer whose works have appeared in numerous magazines and anthologies. Kim and her partner hope to adopt "Tommy."

Leigh Anne Jasheway is a humor writer, stand-up comic, and stress management consultant, in Eugene, Oregon. She draws extensively from her dysfunctional family life in creating healing humor. She writes, for example, "My Mom has been married five times. Not to be outdone, my Dad has also been married five times. Our family photo takes up the whole mantle, and every other person's face is blacked out. . . . Holidays were cheap around our house. We didn't want to spend much on each other because we were pretty sure that come next year we wouldn't even be related." In addition to editing a feminist humor newsletter, *Rags to Bitches*, Jasheway's writing has been published in the *LA Times, Hysteria, Women's Harpoon,* and *Contemporary Comedy*.

Gayle Lauradunn's poems have appeared most recently in *Tsunami, Zone 3, Connecticut River Review, Puerto del Sol,* and in the Sierra Club book, *Mother Earth Through the Eyes of Women Photographers and Writers.* She lives in western Massachusetts where she has recently begun a business offering fundraising training for non-profit organizations.

After working as a gas station manager, sanitorium cook, maid, and donut holer, **Dorianne Laux** moved to Berkeley in 1983, where she began "writing in earnest." When her daughter was 9, she returned to school and worked toward her degree in English from Mills College, which she earned with Honors in 1988. Since then, her poems have appeared in many of the country's top literary journals, and she has had two collections of poetry published by BOA Press, *Awake* (1990), and *What We Carry* (1994), which was nominated for a National Book Critics Circle Award. Currently Laux is on the faculty of the University of Oregon where she teaches Creative Writing between her many cross-country reading engagements.

Allie Light is a filmmaker, teacher, poet, and editor. To date, she has written, produced, and directed eight films with her partner, Irving Saraf. *In the Shadow of the Stars* won the 1991 Academy Award for Best Documentary Feature, and *Dialogues with Madwomen* , directed by Light, won several prizes, including the Freedom of Expression Award at the 1994 Sundance Film Festival. Light has also published a book of poems, *The Glittering Cave,* and edited an anthology of women's writings called *Poetry From Violence.* For ten years she was a lecturer in Women's Studies at San Francisco State University. Her current films in progress are *Rachel's Daughters,* examining the causes of breast cancer, and *Dreamwalkers,* exploring the imaginative worlds of people who are disabled. She has also been invited to co-direct a film about the Fourth World Conference on Women in Beijing in September 1995.

Roseann Lloyd's collection of poetry, now in its second printing, is titled *Tap Dancing for Big Mom* (New Rivers Press, 1986). She co-authored, with Richard Solly, *Journey Notes: Writing for Recovery and Spiritual Growth* (Ballantine 1992). She co-edited, with Deborah Keenan, *Looking for Home: Women Writing about Exile* (Milkweed Editions), which received an American Book Award from the Before Columbus Foundation in 1991.

Rachel Loden's poems have appeared in many magazines, including *New American Writing, College English, New York Quarterly*, and *The Prose Poem*, and are forthcoming in *Seneca Review, Graham House Review, Onthebus, Caliban*, and others. She lives in Palo Alto, California, with her husband and daughter, and works with private poetry students.

Donna Longenecker writes, "In spite of all the good things I've learned to make happen in my life there are still pieces of a past life for which have yet to find a voice. For now they exist in turmoil, darkness—while I go about the routine of living. I've learned that living is a kind of prayer, a movement toward the hope of giving voice to lost things."

Marjorie Maddox has two chapbooks out, *Nightrider to Edinburgh* (Amelia, 1986, winner of the Charles William Duke Long Poem Award), and *How to Fit God Into a Poem* (Painted Bride, 1994, chapbook winner). She was also the winner of *Seattle Review's* Bentley Prize for Poetry and Fiction. Maddox has studied writing with A.R. Ammons and others at Cornell, where she was awarded the Sage Graduate Fellowship in Creative Writing for her M.F.A. At present, she is an Assistant Professor of Literature and Writing at Lock Haven University.

Maria Theresa Maggi is a poet, essayist, and astrologer. Her work has appeared in various journals, magazines, and anthologies, and she teaches writing part-time at the University of Idaho. Her first volume of poems, titled *Rings Around Saturn*, will be published in the Fall of 1995 by Black Rock Press at the University of Nevada. She lives, heals, writes, and watches the sky with her ten-year-old son, Michael, in Moscow, Idaho.

Most recently **Moira Magneson** has been working as the muffin baker at Camp Lotus on the American River in California. Her poems have appeared in several magazines, such as *Fine Madness* and *Five Fingers Review*.

Bella Mahaya is amazed how powerful silence can be, but is even more amazed by the freedom that comes with speaking out. She's writing a novel based on five generations of family secrets, trying to get pregnant, and planning to learn more about non-violent ways to raise children.

Joan Makepeace lives in Cambridge, Massachusetts with her Siamese cat, Tao, (aka Mr. Cat). For the past eight years she has conducted research in learning and creativity, looking at diverse fields such as educational psychology, the fine arts, computer technology, and the humanities. Her personal history as a survivor of childhood physical and sexual abuse is often reflected in her poetry and other artistic pursuits, and has led her to volunteer time working with other abuse survivors.

Paul Scott Malone is the author of *In an Arid Land: Thirteen Stories of Texas* (TCU Press, 1995). A former N.E.A. Fellow, he now serves as a book reviewer for *The Dallas Morning News* and as Corresponding Editor in Fiction for *Writers' Forum*. He lives with his wife, Cheryl, in Wimberley, Texas.

Becky Meyer is twenty-nine years old, and currently working toward her B.A. in English Education at South Dakota State University. She writes that "Prayer of a Young Girl" represents an experiment in content for her: "an exploration into forbidden territory. I found as I worked on this piece that it affected me far more than I imagined possible. I sincerely hope it has the same effect on others who may read it." Although she has been writing for many years, this is the first piece that she has ever submitted for publication.

Homer Mitchell's publication credits include *Southern Review, Small Pond, Blueline,* and *Poetpourri*. He teaches as an adjunct instructor at colleges in Northern New York, and grows over 100 varieties of herbs. Between teaching and writing he enjoys bushwhacking in the Adirondack Mountains.

Patricia Monaghan is the author of two books of poetry: *Winterburning* (Fireweed Press, 1989) and *Seasons of the Witch* (Delphi Press, 1992). She has also written three books of nonfiction. The poem "Knowing the Bomb So Well" is from her work-in-progress, *Homefront*, a collection of poems about the roots of family violence in international conflict. She lives in Chicago.

Gail Morse loves living in Cambridge, Massachusetts with her cat, parrot, and boyfriend. She balances dancing and writing with friends, housework, and supporting local singer-songwriters. She graduated from Rensselaer Polytechnic Institute with a B.S. in psychology, and worked primarily in academic libraries until her decision to write full-time.

Patricia L. Nichol was in the Peace Corps in the Philippines from 1963-1965. In 1979, she received an M.A. in English from California State University at Sacramento. She has taught school for more than twenty years, and has been writing for fifteen. Married for twenty-two years, she has a twenty year-old son. Much of her life has been spent working on recovering from sexual abuse at the hands of her father which lasted from the age of eight months until she was sixteen years old.

Elizabeth Oakley lives and writes in Belmont, California. She earned her M.A. in Creative Writing from San Francisco State University in 1993. Loving open spaces, physicality, and almost any music, she is currently completing a novel and supports herself as both a Junior College composition teacher and P.R./Office Manager for BAMM Impact Self Defense.

Jane Orleman has been a painter for almost half her fifty-some years. In Ellensburg, Washington, she and her husband, artist Dick Elliott, have created an art site which they call *Dick and Jane's Spot*. She considers her paintings a dialogue with herself, and a way to find healing from the memories of childhood abuse which haunted her. Her paintings have been widely displayed and highly acclaimed throughout the United States.

Kathleen Patrick is a poet and fiction writer with an M.A. in Creative and Professional Writing from the University of Minnesota. Her awards include a Loft-McKnight Award, an Honorable Mention from the Academy of American Poets, and a Jerome Foundation Travel Grant. She says "I am the oldest daughter in a family with six children, which in itself explains a lot." She lives in Minnesota with her husband and two young children.

Nita Penfold's poetry has been published in *If I Had My Life to Live Over, I Would Pick More Daisies* (Papier Mache Press); *Love's Shadow,Breaking up is Hard to do* (both Crossing Press); and *Catholic Girls* (Plume\Penguin Books). She writes to speak her truth and to honor the child who survived.

Amanda Powell's poems have appeared in anthologies and journals including *From Here We Speak: Oregon Poetry, The Ardis Anthology of New American Poetry, Ploughshares, Sinister Wisdom, Sojourner,* and *The Women's Review of Books*. She has received numerous grants and awards, among them a residency at the Centrum Foundation in Port Townsend, Washington, the Massachusetts Artists Foundation Fellowship for Poetry, and a National Endowment for the Humanities Translation Fellowship. Her poem, "Freud's Back," included in this anthology, won the 1989 Grolier Prize. Her translations from the Spanish include *Untold Sisters: Hispanic Nuns in Their Own Works*

(16th- to 18th-century poetry and prose; U. New Mexico Press, 1989) and *The Answer/ La respuesta* by Sor Juana Ines de la Cruz (Feminist Press, 1994; with Electa Arenal).

Eve Powers writes, "My recovery from childhood abuse began in 1985. In 1988 I participated in founding a local chapter of a national peer support program for incest survivors, and began speaking about recovery from childhood abuse at professional conferences. Currently a counselor, writer and amateur naturalist living and working in Eugene, Oregon, I work with clients on issues of childhood abuse, healing the inner child, and co-dependency. Since incest and abuse leave deep wounds in soul and spirit, I encourage my clients to cultivate a rich spiritual life of their choice. In writing myths and poems about my experience as a survivor, I break the silence so cruelly forced upon the deepest and truest parts of myself, and re-build my connections with myself and with all of life."

Marjorie Power's poetry has been published in *Living With It* (Wampeter Press) and in many magazines and reviews, including *The Seattle Review, Southern Poetry Review, The New Virginia Review,* and the anthology *Life on the Line* (Negative Capability Press).

Chriss-Spike Quatrone is a writer living in New York. Her poems, short stories, and essays have been published in over fifteen different 'zines (some more than once).

Anne Recker is a full time mother of four, working part–time as a librarian. Recently, she has begun to write. Her first short story for children appeared in *Pocket Magazine* in June 1994. She also writes learning cards for an educational company, Boomerang Book Club in Texas. She wrote her piece, "Maybe God Is an Old Woman," because it's been her experience that abuse is as destructive as any disease, passing from generation to generation as if it were a mutant gene.

Richard E. Reed is an author, literary agent, playwright, performer and poet living in Springfield, Oregon. His latest book, published in the U.S., Great Britain and Germany, is *The Self-Aware Universe*, with Amit Goswami, which explores the spiritual aspects of quantum physics. His radio drama, *Going Crazy* , was broadcast in the spring of 1995 by KLCC. His most recent collection of poetry, *Soul Songs* (Prasad Press, 1995), includes several poems which have been set to music and performed by the Dance Theatre of Oregon. Reed also performs in *The Dick & Bill Show* , exploring inner space with poetry, music and laughter.

Holly Lu Conant Rees is a feminist, Quaker, vegetarian mother of a wondrous eleven year-old. She's had poems published ir

Sojourner, Frontiers and the *Birmingham Poetry Review*. Her paid work is with a parent support network for families who have a child with special needs, as she does.

Bernice Rendrick confronts her family history through the healing process of poetry. She gravitates towards art, music, gardening, and baking bread for the same reason. Although her birth place is Kansas, she now lives in the Santa Cruz area with her husband, Robert. Her poetry has appeared in the anthology, *I am Becoming the Woman I've Wanted*(Papier Mache Press, 1994), and in such periodicals as the *Santa Barbara Review, Kansas Quarterly, Quarry West, Green Fuse,* and others.

Elisavietta Ritchie's *Flying Time: Stories & Half–Stories* includes four PEN Syndicated Fiction winners. Her poetry collections include *The Arc of the Storm; Elegy for the Other Woman: new & selected terribly female poems; A Wound–Up Cat and Other Bedtime Stories; Raking The Snow; Tightening The Circle Over Eel Country*. She is also the editor of *The Dolphin's Arc: Poems on Endangered Creatures of the Sea, Finding The Name,* and other books.

Most of **Emily Robertson**'s poetry is about Love and being Black. She writes, "While I enjoy reliving and creating beautiful erotic moments in my poetry, I also feel strongly that domestic abuse must be discussed and explored." Emily is 23 years old and attends the University of Washington in Seattle. The poems presented here are from her collection, *Afrodisiac.*

Eva Schlesinger's father immigrated to the West Coast when he was 14, and ever since she was 14, she wanted to live there, too. She now lives in the Bay Area where she is a writer and artist.

Jennifer Smith-Morris is twenty-four, married, and has two children. She graduated from Oregon State University in 1993, and now lives in Texas.

David Starkey is the author of several collections of poetry, most recently a chapbook entitled *I Will Not Do Anything Stupid Again* (Palanquin/TDM, 1995). He teaches English at a college in suburban Chicago.

Anne Stilwell grew up in the Sierra Nevada mountains of California, where she lived in the woods and in books and began writing at age ten. Since then, she has lived in Montana, Spain, and Oregon. Her work has appeared in *Feminist Broadcast Quarterly.*

Susanna J. Sturgis's writing in a variety of genres is most in-uenced by growing up in an alcoholic family and living in artha's Vineyard. If she weren't a lesbian feminist, she wouldn't able to make sense of any of it.

Nancy Takacs lives in rural Utah near Price with her husband, son, and two dogs. She teaches Creative Writing and English at the College of Eastern Utah, where she also directs a poetry and fiction reading series.

Cheryl A. Townsend was a volunteer with the Akron Rape Crisis Center and continues to work with local police authorities. She edits *Impetus* magazine, is the House Poet for Borders Books and hosts a poetry radio show on WAPS in Akron, Ohio.

Lequita Vance-Watkins received a 1993 California Artists Fellowship for Literature, and was a Djerassi Foundation Resident Artist alternate for 1995. Her poetry and interviews appear in a wide variety of journals and anthologies. She is the co-editor and translator of *White Flash/Black Rain*, an anthology of writings by Japanese women about the bombing of Hiroshima and Nagasaki (Milkweed Editions, 1995) released in time to commemorate the fifty year anniversary of the bombing.

Jeff Walt was raised in Pennsylvania and received his M.F.A. from Goddard College in Vermont, where he worked with Mark Doty, Michael Klein, and Nora Mitchell. Most recently, his poems have appeared in the anthology, *Gents, Bad Boys, and Barbarians*, and he was awarded a fellowship to attend a two-week Writing Studio session at the Vermont Studio Center. His recently-completed book-length manuscript of poems, *Orogeny*, details "the uncommon violence of childhood and the redemption of surviving your own life."

Therese Anne Ward married at sixteen. Her husband, Dan, was twenty. She says that she has "had a life intermixed with struggle, pain, happiness and lots of change and growth." She and Dan enjoy three daughters, two sons, six grandchildren, and a great-grandchild as they celebrate their thirty-seventh anniversary. Therese writes that Yoga, supplementing a Roman Catholic upbringing, was the path of her journey toward healing and wholeness, which also led her through a B.S. in Psychology, private therapy and twelve-step work. Today, she is a licensed massage therapist in private practice. Her window on life is Unity in Diversity—the Oness of ALL.

Jackie Warren-Moore is a poet, playwright, columnist and director who lives in Syracuse, New York. In 1975 she published her first book of poems, *Change Chilly to Cold*, and saw her first play produced. Since then her poems and short stories have appeared nationally in little magazines, her work was included in Charlotte Watson Sherman's 1994 anthology, *Sisterfire*, and she has completed a new manuscript entitled *Ms. Mean*. Besides directing for the Paul Robeson Performing Arts Company, she has had her plays, *Freedom's Stone: The Jerry Rescue Story* (1989) and *Father's Day* (1990), produced by that company, and she is now at work on an historical play. Long associated with the Community Writers' Project, she has conducted many readings and poetry workshops in the Syracuse schools, for senior citizens, and in numerous colleges, prisons and psychiatric centers. She is a regular columnist for the Syracuse *Herald-American* and writes reviews for the *Quarterly Black Review of Books*. She is married and has four daughters and a grandson.

Kennette Harrison Wilkes writes, "The mother who battered and abused me when she was her 'other self,' is the same mother who jumped up in the sedate audience and shouted like a cheer leader when I got my M.A. in Creative Writing after having attended classes in a reclining lawn chair at middle age while suffering from a debilitating illness. Writing has been my best medicine."

Gary Young's most recent books are *The Dream of a Moral Life* and *Wherever I Looked*. He has received fellowships from the National Endowment for the Arts, and the National Endowment for the Humanities, and was recently awarded a grant from the Vogelstein Foundation and a Pushcart Prize. He is editor of Greenhouse Review Press, and his print work is represented in numerous collections including the Museum of Modern Art, New York, the Victoria and Albert Museum, London, and special collection libraries throughout the country. He lives with his wife and son in the mountains north of Santa Cruz, California.

Claudia Yukman says, "I find myself trying to make family with strangers. For me, poetry is speaking to strangers, exploring what it might be possible to say. I've been teaching poetry and poetics for ten years, both in the community and at the university. The poets who speak to me the most are Hopkins, Dickinson, Whitman, Stevens, Rich, and H.D. I am also listening hard to poets writing now."

PUBLICATION ACKNOWLEDGMENTS

Grateful acknowledgment is made to the following publications which first published or accepted for publication some of the material in this book.

Laure-Anne Bosselaar's "The Bumper Sticker" was anthologized in *Drive They Said, Poems about Americans and their Cars* (Milkweed Editions, 1994). "The Cellar" appeared in the *Massachusetts Review*, and "From My Windows, I See Mountains" was published in *The Writer's Path* (Iowa Press, 1995). Jeanne Bryner's poem, "Candles," won an honorable mention and was published in *The Denny Poems Anthology 1991-92*. Elizabeth Claman's poem, "Good-Bye to the Dust Jacket Satyr," was published in *Bastard Review* 5/6 (1993). Joan Dobbie's "Yoga Class: The Teacher Speaks" appeared in *Heaven Bone* (1987) and *Healing Currents* (1991). A slightly different version of Sue Doro's piece, "Father Poems: Coming to Grips with the Past," was published in *Liberating Memory, Our Work and Our Working-Class Consciousness*, edited by Janet Zandy (Rutgers University Press, 1994), and appears here with permission of the author. Frances Driscoll's poem "Night Dance," was previously published in *Hollins Critic* and in *Talk to Me*, a chapbook published by Black River Press. W.D. Ehrhart's poem, "The Simple Lives of Cats," appeared first in *Poet Lore* (Winter 1991-92). Susan Eisenberg's "Anger Guidelines" was first published in *Embers*. Karl Elder's poem, "Dawn Run," was previously published in *Slant* (1993). Molly Fisk's poem, "Veterans," won the first prize in the National Writers' Union Competition, judged by Adrienne Rich, and was published in *Love's Shadow*, edited by Amber Coverdale Sumrall (Crossing Press, 1993); "Daughters" appeared in the *Haight Ashbury Review*. Fisk's interview with Louise Wisechild was previously published in *The Healing Woman*, January 1995. "Mother," by John Gilgun was previously published in *Amethyst: A Journal for Lesbians and Gay Men* (1990), and in *What's Become of Eden: Poems of Family* (Slapering Hol Press, 1994). Quinton Hallett's poem "At Ease" previously appeared in the chapbooks, *Inscape*, and*Quarry*, both 1992, "Shooting Stars" was in *Fireweed*, in January 1993. M. Eliza Hamilton's poem, "The Place Where I Am," appears under a different title in the revised edition of *Chain, Chain, Change: For Black Women Dealing with Physical and Emotional Abuse*, edited by Evelyn C. White (Seal Press, 1995). "Robert's Affair," by Richard Hine was included in the Summer 1994 issue of *Loyalhanna Review*. Dorianne Laux's four poems, "Two Pictures of My Sister," "What My Father Told Me," "Quarter to Six," and "The Tooth Fairy," were all previously published in *Awake* (BOA, 1993). Rachel Loden's "A Falling Woman" first appeared in the *Cumberland Review*, "Praise of Darkness" in *Thirteenth Moon*, "The Castle" in *Southern Poetry Review*, and "Archaeology (As If the Past Mattered)" in the *Midwest Quarterly*. Donna Longenecker's poem, "Semper Fi," was previously included in the anthology, *Sixteen Voices: Poets: Survivors of Incest and Sexual Abuse*, edited by Joe Mowery (Mariposa Press, 1994). Jane Orleman's painting, "Beyond All Reason," previously appeared in *The Sun, A Magazine* (May 1992), and *Arterial* 2, (1992); "If Looks Could Kill" and "Symptoms of Child Abuse" were published in *Sojourner* (Vol. 17, no. 2, 1992), and *Journey* (Vol. 4, no. 2, 1992); "Damned Daddy" appeared in *Calyx* (Vol. 13, no. 3, 1991) and in *Sojourner* (Vol. 17, no. 6, 1992). Amanda Powell's poem, "Freud's Back," was the winner of a Grolier prize. Richard Reed's two poems, "Look at Me," and "The Day Dad Shrank," are reprinted from *Soul Songs* (Prasad, 1995). Bernice Rendrick's "Waking My Parents," appeared in the chapbook, *Voices and Visions II* (Wordshop, 1994). "Stable Tales" was published in *Her Wits About Her* (Harper Collins, 1987); reprinted in *Flying Time: Stories And Half–Stories* (Signal Books, 1992), and appears here with permission from author, Elisavietta Ritchie. Nancy Takacs' "Pontiac" first appeared in *Weber Studies* (vol. 12, Winter 1995). An abbreviated version of "Daughters" by Jackie Warren-Moore appeared in *Sisterfire: Black Womanist Fiction and Poetry*, edited by Charlotte Watson Sherman (HarperPerennial, 1994). "Dear Mother, I Want to Forgive," by Kinnette Harrison Wilkes, was included in the anthology, *Life on the Line: Selections of Words & Healing*, edited by Sue Walker (Negative Capability). Gary Young's poem, "My father would say . . ." originally appeared in the *New England Review;* "Sleight of Hand" was published in *Hands* (Illuminati Press, 1979); and "My mother loved violets" first appeared in the *Denver Quarterly*.